Goose River Anthology, 2023

Edited by

Deborah J. Benner

Goose River Press
Waldoboro, Maine

Library of Congress Card Number: 2023945373

ISBN: 978-1-59713-262-6 paperback
ISBN: 978-1-59713-263-3 hard cover

First Printing, 2023

Cover photo by Melissa Winslow Olson.

Published by
Goose River Press
3400 Friendship Road
Waldoboro, ME 04572
email: gooseriverpress@gmail.com
www.gooseriverpress.com

Authors Included

Authors Included

Authors Included

In Memory of
our dear friend
Jean M. B. Lawrence

Special thanks to Sue Campagna for her wonderful help in proofing the book.

Goose River Anthology, 2023

Don Bouwens
Portland, ME

A Wicked Close Call

I moved to Maine in 1972. My challenge was to use a workhorse to skid logs from my friend's woodlot. Unlike bulldozers or skidders, horses need just a narrow path which soon grows back leaving no trace. But I had never harnessed, let alone owned a horse of any kind.

Local friend Keith suggested I contact Fred who cut pulp on his woodlot using a horse as I planned to do. I introduced myself to this kind farmer asking if I could help him for a week, working for free, just to observe and learn. The way he worked with his horse, Jess, was a thing of beauty. Fred would cut a few fir trees, limb them, back Jess up, hook a chain around the butt ends, attach it to the grab hook on the harness's whiffle tree, tell her to "walk ahead," and she would calmly amble down the path to the roadside "yard" and wait for Fred to come unhook the load and start her back for another trip. She would walk to the end of the path and wait for Fred to come and cut the next load.

If only I had had Fred's experience and demeanor and found a horse like Jess.

Keith's next referral was to someone who could help me find a horse to purchase. He sent me to Earl Worcester, a widower who lived nearby in the village. Most Mainers spend a fair amount of time beating around a few bushes before getting to the point of a conversation...the weather, the crops, the Red Sox, etc. I found Earl behind his house in his vegetable garden with a hoe in his hand, sweating on a hot day in his "wife-beater" undershirt. When he saw me approach, his first booming words were, "What the hell do you want?" And thus began one of my most treasured friendships Downeast.

Earl was a big man. Tall, bald, with a heavy body...not fat, just very stout. He had made his livelihood buying and

Don Bouwens
Portland, ME

selling livestock. I'm guessing that as a younger man he was as strong as some of the bulls he handled. When we first met, he was seventy-eight, fifty-two years my senior. I told Earl I wanted to buy a workhorse and hoped he would help me. Before long, we were traveling hundreds of miles stopping at places he thought might have a horse to sell.

Earl's firsthand experience in this part of the state was impressive. It seemed that every half mile he shared some personal anecdote: "I used to buy butter from a woman in that house until one day I found a big black hair in the butter...never stopped there again." Or, "That place used to be a pig farm, and I always went there for piglets." Or, "Up on the right they always had horses...let's pull in there, just up that dirt row-ud." Road in Washington County is pronounced row-ud, don't you know. And Earl would sometimes call me "dear," pronounced dee-ah. Some Downeast colloquialisms were entirely new to me, such as this one of older men calling young men "dear." Others new to me were "wicked" (extremely), "tunk" (tap), as in "just tunk it a little," and "ugly" (irritable). Pulling away from one of our stops, Earl asked me if I didn't agree that the woman was "some ugly."

Eventually, we found what Earl thought was a horse that would suit me, a Belgian. Bob was a beautiful horse, but too spirited for woods' work. I tried and tried to get him to just calmly "walk along" like Fred's mare, but Bob would either go full speed ahead or not at all. I tried exhausting him by hitching him to an enormous log to pull along a field road where he couldn't hurt me, but when he started, I couldn't slow him down, even sawing hard on the reins until he stopped dead in his tracks, stubbornly unwilling to move at all, despite my effort to keep him going and tire him out. Then, after catching his breath, he would charge ahead once more.

I got plenty of advice from well-wishers: "He needs to know who's boss...hit him over the head with a 2'x4' " or "He's too full of spirit from the oats you're feeding him...back off the grain and just let him eat hay." Nothing worked.

Don Bouwens
Portland, ME

A city boy, I had never been to a county fair, where they have pulling contests for workhorses. Having since watched these events, though much too late for me and Bob, I now know exactly what the problem was. My horse must have been entered in the contests where the animal is hitched to an extremely heavy load and expected to haul it from one end of the arena to the other in the least amount of time. At a signal, the owner hollers or whips his horse to pull as far and fast as it can until it stops to catch its breath, then off again with all its might. Just like Bob. I suppose, had I known, I might have patiently taught Bob to just walk along by holding his bridle and walking calmly and quietly beside him. But that wasn't in my limited playbook.

I eventually tried using Bob in the woods a few times that fall when the forest floor is covered with noisy leaves and brush. The last time, while I was behind, hooking the load, he nervously kicked back. I felt the wind of a huge steel-clad hoof as it whipped by my cheek. Had he connected, since no one knew my schedule or location, my skeleton might still be in those woods.

Bob did, however, excel at one task that was truly delightful. He could trot along endlessly pulling a heavy rubber-tired farm cart. I can tell you that clip-clopping down a shady country road on a warm fall day, pulled by a handsome Belgian is "wicked nice."

Dorothy Hopkins
Waldoboro, ME

The Things That Came Home

The box arrives to end a four-month wait.
With trembling fingers, I unseal the lid.
An acrid odor—mold and jungle rot—
Wafts out to spread across the living room.
First out a flashlight, cooking gear, a fork,
a spoon, canteen, a folding knife. These things
All issue. Are they your personal effects?

Some books all paperbacks with covers gone
And pages torn, no sign of ownership.
A book of poems I sent, now set aside
To later read and reconnect with you.
Your wallet holds your driver's license,
ID and nine piasters, but all the photos
I knew you carried were carefully removed.

Some coins, a pen knife, where the letters I sent?
I hold a poncho liner close to see
If I can catch your scent, but none remains,
so fold to wash and use upon my bed.
This box reminds me of the emptiness
that stretches forth without you in my life.
The scent of Vietnam lingers in the room.

Bill Herring
Minnetonka, MN

Daydream, Tenth Grade English Lit

Mr. Ethington opened the book,
cleared his throat and began to read:
Whan that Aprille with his shoures soote,
The droghte of March hath perced to the roote
And bathed every veyne in swich licóur...

And under the weight of those lines
my attention began to crumble,
turning from the bespectacled balding man
at the front of the class
to the raven-haired Sharon
two desks to my left,
those legs, hem of skirt an inch or two
above the knees,
and I was no longer listening
to the drone of Chaucer,
but instead found myself lost
in a soft focus daydream
where we're slow dancing
at the Val Air, mirror ball
stirring much more than the ceiling,
Temptations singing
I've got sunshine on a cloudy day...

And half a life later here we are,
empty nesters slow dancing across
the living room floor
because dreams can be timeless.
As timeless as love.

Liz Mockler
Newport, ME

Homework

I spend most of my day
in one room,
like a freed convict
unable to leave.

Most everything I need
is in that one room,
waiting for a dust rag
when I feel up to it.

I seldom ever do though,
because the house never
looks as bad as I feel.

That's when I'll know
to get the rag,
when I feel better
than the house looks.

***

Sylvia Little-Sweat
Wingate, NC

Jubilee

Teaching sixty years—
Mining diamonds in the rough,
Polishing facets

Ilga Winicov Harrington
Falmouth, ME

Baiting Bear at Midnight

All good fairy tales start: "Long ago and far away when the world was new." The world is always new when one is young, long ago is relative to one's age, and far away could be the next town if one has never traveled. Such tales often depict the impetuosity of youth that counts the cost of improbable activity only as an afterthought. This is a story of an evening that could very well be a fairy tale.

Long ago, more than a half a century, on a very late and steamy evening in June, dusk lingered over the street near the Midwest university. Ingelore and Samet strolled out of the small corner restaurant on a tree-lined street skirting the campus. The neighborhood place was one of their favorites boasting red checkered tablecloths, each topped with an old Chianti wine bottle, stubbed candle and dripping wax, with grapes dangling from trellised vines over each booth. Warm and inviting to everyone, true to its Tuscan name on the dim sign out front. They had gone to a movie earlier and lingered over a glass of wine after their pizza, a luxury given their graduate student stipends. Certainly, a contrast to their weekdays, crammed full of classes, along with part time jobs to make ends meet. It was a time when girls wore poodle skirts and bobby socks, and a young man would dress in fresh khakis and a white shirt to take a girl out on a Saturday night.

The sun had long set, but the evening twilight still set a soft glow. They stepped out in the lingering heat of the day. The street had quieted down from its earlier bustle, and they stopped a few steps away from the restaurant.

"What now?" asked Samet.

"We could take a walk down to Mendota," suggested Ingelore.

"Sounds good. How about we stop and pick up ice cream

Ilga Winicov Harrington
Falmouth, ME

on the way to the lake?"

"I'm full, but something cold would be good."

As they continued down the street, they talked about classes and people at the university. Though they spent their days in different buildings on the campus, they shared several friends between them. They laughed at some prank one of Samet's friends had managed in class the week before. The pair had dated on and off for a while and were comfortable with each other.

They soon came to the ice cream stand at the next corner. The guy dishing out scoops was wearing a baggy Bucky Badger shirt and a satisfied smile. The heat was good for his business, and he was staying open much later than usual. Students and others were still out walking, trying to catch an elusive breeze off the lake, before reluctantly returning to their stifling dorm rooms or apartments. Air conditioning was still reserved for movies and only some high-class restaurants, leading anyone who could, to head outdoors on such a steamy night.

Samet chose vanilla, Ingelore her usual strawberry, and with glistening sugar cones in hand, they proceeded down to the lakeshore. The dwindling light shimmered above the calm waters of the lake. Occasionally, a whisper of a breeze would ripple the tall grass at its edge. It was a good time for reflection as they gazed out over the water, trying to keep up with the rapidly melting ice cream cones.

It was Ingelore's first year away from home and she was still adapting to her independence. She had left East Coast city life the previous fall and found it fascinating to be living in a small Midwest university town. No more subways, trams, and buses. Everything here seemed to be so much closer, you could walk to almost everywhere. There were three lakes and adjacent parks, one even with a small zoo, all within the town proper. But the winter had been very cold, with bitter gusts of wind across this very lake making the daily walk to the university an icy experience.

Ilga Winicov Harrington
Falmouth, ME

Grad school was interesting, but she missed her friends back home, some of whom she had known all her life. Though letters arrived regularly from them and her family, she was glad to be away from her very strict parents. It was a weight lifted from her shoulders that she no longer needed to always heed their expectations for serious and ladylike manners. She often shared in letters, with her childhood friend back home, her newfound discoveries of many simple pleasures in life full of laughter and daring. She found she relished impromptu activities for just the fun of it! Now she wondered about Samet who was always so preoccupied.

"What are you thinking about, Samet?" she blurted out as she took another lick of her cone.

"Umm, guess I was thinking of next week's experiments." Samet spent his days in the chemistry department and needed always to come up with new ways to solve his thesis problems in synthesis of organic molecules.

Ingelore shook her head and grinned. It was just like Samet to be always focused and serious. Sometimes she wished she could shake up some of those formulas and chemical reactions in Samet's head just to make him smile. They needed something to dispel this aura of predictability.

"Have you seen the bear in Vilas Park?"

Samet shook his head. "No, I haven't. Where did that come from?"

"I bet there isn't any breeze at all behind his bars in the zoo."

"Probably not." Confused he asked, "Why so concerned about the bear?"

"It's hot! I just feel sorry for him."

"And...where is this conversation going?" Samet raised an eyebrow. "Is this going to be another one of your quests?"

"Well, we could take him an ice cream cone..." Ingelore mused.

"Are you out of your mind?"

"No, it is quite doable. Vilas Park is small, and I've taken walks there in the evening including visits to the small zoo. It is close to my rooming house and sometimes I like to walk in the evening."

"You *are* out of your mind!"

"Not at all," said Ingelore as she chewed her bottom lip. Her mind was already racing. "The small zoo is not behind locked gates. You can go there anytime, day or night. We can get another ice cream cone, hop in your car and be there in just a few minutes."

"No way! You will drip ice cream all over my car!" Samet groused and emphatically shook his head. "I just washed and vacuumed it this morning," he added drawing out the words, but Ingelore could see he was weakening.

"Nonsense, I'll take lots of extra napkins. Let's go," she said dragging him by the sleeve.

Shortly, they were back at the ice cream shack, but the guy in the Bucky Badger shirt was already closing up.

"Wait," pleaded Ingelore, "we need another cone."

The guy stopped pulling down the front closure, winked and said, "You really must have liked that strawberry cone."

"Hmmm...no, I'll have vanilla this time," Ingelore shook her head, "and please give me lots and lots of extra napkins."

Samet quietly grumbling said nothing as they turned and returned to the car. The green Plymouth was hot, but once they got going, the breeze from the open windows quickly made it pleasant. Ingelore clutched a fistful of napkins and kept an eye on the ice cream, taking a couple of small licks from the dripping cone until they arrived at the park.

They parked on grass near a path through a stand of pine into the tiny zoo and followed a narrow winding path to '*their*' bear. It had grown dark, but the moon was just rising over the horizon in the gap between the park trees. An owl hooted from a large oak up ahead. They had left the street-light behind them. They continued toward the shallow embankment and there it was, the bear enclosure, high-walled and filled with craggy boulders, the full moon now sufficient to follow the path. Another solitary bird called in the distance, but otherwise silence. They moved ahead without speaking.

As they approached an almost two-story open cage, Ingelore and Samet could see the dark furry shape of the bear, lying close to the bars in front. He seemed asleep. In fact, he appeared to be snoring as regular puffs of air came from his mouth with an occasional snout snuffle. Ingelore leaned over the three-foot railing that separated visitors from the actual cage extending her hand toward the bars. Too far, there was at least a three-foot gap between the cone and the bars. She leaned as far as she was able, standing on the tips of her toes, but it was still too far to reach the cage from where she was standing. Ingelore took another lick of the dripping cone and without a thought, climbed over the railing. Samet gasped a choking breath. The bear slept on.

With her back as close to the railing as she could manage, Ingelore leaned forward extending her arm with the cone toward the bear. It took a couple of wiggles until the vanilla-flavored treat rested between two bars with her holding the very bottom of the cone. Her shoulder ached from the stretched position. Ingelore held her breath, two more snuffles escaped from the bear. *Did she need to call the bear*? Suddenly, the cone was ripped out of her hand. It was gone so fast, Ingelore barely managed a swallowed screech. She heaved back against the railing with heart pounding. Gathering her breath she scrambled back over the railing not daring to look back at the enclosure. When she finally did, there was no sign of the cone. But there was some movement. The bear's eyes shone black in the moonlight, as he busily licked the bars for any remaining trace of ice cream.

"Satisfied?" Sammet's tone was notably sarcastic as he shook his head.

The walk back to the car was quiet but welcome since serious concentration was needed for Ingelore to make her still wobbly legs function on the gravel path.

Ilga Winicov Harrington
Falmouth, ME

The speed at which all that had happened! In a split second the cone was gone! How close had the bear's claws been to her hand? Yet she had felt nothing beside the cone being yanked away. Had any of that matted fur brushed against her? She inspected her hand, but could see nothing in the dark.

Samet walked beside her with an occasional string of unintelligible words muttered under his breath. Conversation seemed to have disappeared from between them. He later dropped her at her rooming house, where they parted with a very quiet "good night."

Ingelore barely managed to get upstairs to her room. She was still shaking as she leaned her back against the closed door and took a deep breath. The clock in her landlady's apartment chimed midnight. She listened to the chimes and looked at the familiar backyard through her window, the lone apple tree lighted now by the risen moon. The view had remained as other nights, quiet and serene, except for her still rapid heartbeat signaling some change. The evening had certainly sparked considerable excitement with her dare to feed the bear. It had fortunately ended with only a quiet "good night." Now, on reflection, she had to acknowledge that *'daring'* might need a dash of *'sense'* for her future quests.

Ingelore would occasionally think of that evening afterwards. She wondered if on sultry summer nights the bear would look longingly at his bars, expecting another magical cold treat to appear there near midnight. She did not share her thoughts on this with Samet. He would only tell her that it was her fanciful imagination getting her carried away. Samet himself, afterwards, never mentioned the events of that evening.

However, on her next visit home, her best childhood friend with whom she had shared the story in a letter, greeted her with an amused and expectant look on his face.

His first words were, "Fed any more bears lately?"

Emily Blair Stribling
Brooklin, ME

Returning

They bought the house in late August
just as the light began to fade,
as tomatoes still on the vine
surrendered their sweetness,
as golden rod scorched meadows,
as fires were kindled
to warm chilly mornings.

They moved in early November
well aware that this far north
this time of year, light ebbs
flowing back into a sea of darkness,
compressing days into no more
than knobs that open drawers
full of night and stars.

By December they were settled back
into this village on the coast of Maine
as if they'd never left,
trusting the light would return
just as they had,
in time to grab the brass ring,
a chance to live a radiant life.

Thomas Peter Bennett
Silver Spring, MD

Woodpecker Routine

The Downy Woodpecker,
        after a flurry
of morning activity,
        enlarging its
hollow in the Wild Cherry's branch,
        glanced at the balcony
feeder on the nearby brick building.

The feeder had just been refilled.
Hopefully, more sunflower seeds!

The smallest of woodpeckers,
        a male with a tuft
of red feathers on the back of its head,
        glided down to the feeder
and began tasting and gorging.

Startled, he glanced down.
        A squirrel was fast
climbing the feeder pole.
        The Downy flew
back to the Cherry Tree.

Rebecca Brooks
Topsham, ME

Stand the Watch

I served with honorable men
and women.
Still, you won't see me adorned
with medals and ribbons.
Just honest paint
and a simple light.
We protected each other
through treacherous times,
and guarded against formidable foes,
who hunted the shoals and deep.
My sailors faced onslaughts
at dawn and twilight.
I would illuminate their passage
away from the Atlantic Graveyard.
Steadfast, they called me.
For one-hundred forty-eight years;
unyielding to the storms.
Yet Neptune and his forces
gave cause for my defense.
So my comrades took charge
and restationed me away from harm.
I need no shiny trinkets
to prove my worth.
I stood the watch
with a brilliant glow.

M. Macy
South Bristol, ME

Inheritance

When I go to Molly's house
to sit in wicker by the sea,
I find myself pulled on by porches
and held by what would be
if time were made of rocking chairs
set to motion by the sun.

It is there in harmony with teacups,
writing desks, and rose-hip jam
that geraniums tell beach plums
the secret that I am
undone by seashells—

and that life was once a gentler time;
a sundial-fashioned dream to be
handed down as fine bone china
wrapped in bombazine

when Grandfather knew
the blue
of Ageratum.

Gerry Di Gesu
West Chatham, MA

MR. B.

I approached the Boy Scout leader with apprehension, my mind cluttered with the resentment I sometimes felt when I needed someone to help my son. The noisy, boisterous swirl of Boy Scouts in the room reinforced my feeling that I was making a mistake by enrolling Kevin in the troop. His Cub Scout years had been spent with a den mother who was an understanding friend. Since my husband's work schedule didn't allow him to participate in Scout activities, now Kevin would be with indifferent strangers.

Mr. B. listened quietly as I explained Kevin's learning disabilities, severe asthma, and the fact he was always the "goat" in any group, never accepted by his peers. I disliked asking for special consideration for him, but years of experience had taught me it was best to be honest with people I hoped would be able to help him grow and mature.

"He'll be okay, dearie. You just run along now and pick him up when the meeting's over." Mr. B. smiled gently, patting my arm as he peered at me over the rim of his glasses. I didn't believe him.

"Mr. B.," Gerry Batchelder has been the scoutmaster of Troop 68 at Connecticut Farms Church in Union, NJ, for more than twenty years. He's fostered the growth of a countless number of boys, but I'm sure he hasn't done a better job with anyone than he has with my two sons. He, more than anyone, through example, "friendly persuasion," and his quiet way, has helped them to become fine young men. As their friend and scout leader, he imbued in them a sense of responsibility and loyalty that I still find surprising. Their dedication to him is complete. Eight years is a long time—the years between 10 and 18 when a boy is developing into a young man and his world is changing daily. Those are the years he's been there to guide my boys.

Gerry Di Gesu
West Chatham, MA

Soon Kevin was selling candy and light bulbs to raise money for the troop, enjoying himself at holiday parties and helping out at paper and aluminum drives. "It's okay, Mom. Mr. B. will be there," was the reassurance he gave me whenever he saw the familiar worried look on my face. There were still hassles with some boys who considered him the oddball, but Mr. B. explained Kevin's problems and for the first time he became part of a group.

Since his chronic asthma was severely aggravated by cold weather, Kevin had stayed close to home during the winter months. Now he became involved in the Klondike Derby, an all-day outdoor competition in midwinter among the troops from the Watchung Council. "I have to help Mr. B.," he grinned as he bundled up and hurried out the door. For the first time, Kevin spent a weekend away from home on a Scout camping trip. "I'll just take my pills and I'll be fine, Mom. Don't worry about it." What magic did this man work with my son?

The spring after Kevin joined the troop, Mr. B. and I stood at the back of town hall waiting for the Township Committee meeting to begin. The scouts marched in to present the colors and lead the opening exercises. "Salute," Kevin beamed proudly as he shouted the word. To my stutterer who had special education assistance and speech therapy for years, this one word uttered before an audience was a monumental step.

Mr. B., clad in his red jacket and standing a distance from me, nodded and winked in his impish way, "I told you so," written across the grin on his face. With one success story behind him, was he ready for Christopher?

"I'm not wearing that monkey suit for anybody and I don't want to be a stupid Boy Scout," Chris ranted as he got ready for his first scout meeting. Although gifted in many ways, he projected a false bravado and an "I don't care" attitude to hide his gentleness and insecurities.

Before long, though, Chris was responding to Mr. B.

Gerry Di Gesu
West Chatham, MA

without even being aware of it. Fiercely competitive, he sold extra candy for fundraisers, collected donations for the cancer fund and culminated his achievements by signing up the largest number of sponsors for the annual ten-mile Victory Hike. By raising the most money of any scout in the Watchung Council, he won first prize—the television set which still sits in his room.

Neither Chris nor Kevin seemed able to recount what was discussed in their lengthy conversations with Mr. B. "Nothing much," was the usual answer, but I noted a growing respect for the man, an eager willingness to volunteer and help whenever he needed an extra hand. "Mr. B. needs us, Mom." That was it.

Chris was an usher at church for Scout Sunday, participated in the Flag Day ceremony, and marched in the Memorial Day parade. My shy introvert was now proud to wear his uniform. He rose through the ranks and was on his way toward becoming an Eagle Scout.

Mr. B. was there when Chris went to summer camp, offering encouragement and support. He took him to counselors' homes in order to pass various merit badge tests. He helped him organize special projects and kept pushing and encouraging him to reach within himself to discover all he could be.

Two years ago my mom and mother-in-law became bedridden with cancer. For those two years, Mr. B. was there. He drove the boys to and from meetings and all special activities. A secure haven for them, he often stopped for pizza or burgers on the way home. He was there, listening, loving, and trying to help them understand the confusion and grief they felt.

Often he shared a cup of coffee with my husband and me. Although we talked many hours, I never really got to know him. A shy, private man, his goodness and actions spoke for him.

In June, Chris became an Eagle Scout. As I look at the

Gerry Di Gesu
West Chatham, MA

proud, smiling faces in the snapshots taken that night, I whisper a silent thank you to Mr. B. for helping my sons draw upon inner resources they never realized they possessed to enable them to grow and become all they could be.

***

Erine Leigh
Portsmouth, NH

McGee

Reflections of battered pine
Deflected by the glaze of sea
As the hypnosis of this isle
Settles over me.

The stride of tire-tread cirrus,
A quilt lumped on horizon's bed.
Breakers, like skipping stones,
Layer the vast southwest.

Fragile as a dried urchin,
Strong as the pull of oars,
Legendary as eons of passage,
Momentary as the fatal tick of time.

A crow explodes, cawing.
Above floats the face of moon.
She paints, pastels and shading,
Ever eternal, ebb and flow,

Then rainbow ebb again.

Steve Troyanovich
Florence, NJ

... like moons in a river

When they smile... your eyes...
like moons in a river

—Badr Shakir al-Sayyab

seeping into the threads
of tomorrow's sky
the warmth of your eyes
cradle my unraveling dreams...
somewhere your hands
perfume the tattered fragments
of another tangled dawn

***

sunset lullaby

for Elizabeth

I saw a star behind your eyes

—Bennett Wilson Poole

through your eyes
tender darkness
brings the music
of night—
weary days
forever lost
in exploding colors...

Kate Kearns
Scarborough, ME

To the Garden

Dear dirty obligation,
I set out to want you,
your litany of weeds
green for tending,
those quiet minutes, mist
sizzling from the spigot.
Roses flaunt their pruning
while grateful worms
churn rot to flourishing.
Broccoli popsicles with
your dinner plate leaves,
I meant to love the work
of you the way a poet should.
Brutal beet and carrot
plume, I don't need you
to teach me patience.
I've a sturdy root—Mom
lushed our apartment
windows with succulents
and green ponytails.
Dad named his plants,
lit them from below to
snake shadows up his walls.
You're the first ground
I've owned, though I don't
really. Roma tomato,
that sweet grass tang,
belongs not to this but
to my childhood yard,
to the Italian landlords
who edged the property
with beds and once a year

(continued)

Kate Kearns
Scarborough, ME

filled bins and bins with
fleshy red, blanched
and peeled, performed
their marinara ritual.
I watched them. The way
attention so predictably
brought seedling, to vine,
to pulpy heirlooms year
after year. Listen, I'm still
out here, feet wet with soil.
I'm trying to love you.
It'd be so easy to love you.

***

Margaret Roncone
Vashon, WA

My Slung-Bellied Heart

My heart slung-bellied
drags against wet earth
mud-caked shoes

wind rains down
the eaves of our unfinished
conversation

you become the second
alphabet of misunderstanding

even my mother tongue
loses meaning
love, what fist of stars
will open your door?

Judith Thyng
South Portland, ME

Blueberries and My Grandmother's Tin

Fields covered in blue
Tin pail swinging at my side
Sundrenched days pregnant with
Smells that come alive

The sweetness of pine
Mounds of uneven earth
Crumbling stonewalls hold
A small animal's birth

Wildflowers that garland the grass
Bring a smile to my wandering ways
Little bare feet and sundress too
Stained in wild blueberries and dew

I roam alone and sing
As I fill my tin again
Aloneness is my friend
So my mother said
Yet I don't mind

I have blueberries and my grandmother's tin

Marilyn Weymouth Seguin
Akron, OH

A Thanksgiving Story

Plymouth, Massachusetts 1621

It is late November and the air smells of leaf mold, smoke and sunshine. I adjust my cap so I can feel the warmth of the sun on my face. All around us is the food that we are ready to share. There are fifty of us Pilgrims at the table, and almost twice as many of our Native friends. Our feast is bountiful.

From the forest wilderness—cranberries, nuts and sweet potatoes, venison, turkeys and waterfowl.

From the sea—lobster, eel, crab and cod.

From our own gardens—beans, squash and corn.

Grace is said aloud by one person—our governor, the man who is the leader of our settlement. I want to speak too. I look at my mother, who is silently mouthing her own prayer of gratitude for this bountiful feast. I want to express great gratitude to our Native friends, especially Squanto, who taught us how to find the nuts and berries and how to harvest the fish from the sea. But most important, Squanto taught us how to plant and grow corn that will sustain us through the coming winter. This year's harvest was huge.

My name is Eliza and I am 10 years old.

We arrived in Plymouth last year and that first winter we survived on the food we carried with us aboard the *Mayflower*. There was scarcely enough to eat and we were hungry. More than half of us died that first winter.

We prayed that God would look in our direction and sweep through with a mighty burst of light. And He did. One day in the early spring, Squanto arrived at our settlement. Squanto came from the Wampanoag tribe and was a member of the Patuxet band.

"I speak English," he said, much to our surprise. And that was when the lessons began.

Marilyn Weymouth Seguin
Akron, OH

Squanto taught us how to plant our crop without any plowing or tilling of the hard rocky land. We planted corn, beans, and squash in the Native way, not in rows as we had planted our crops in Europe. The corn was planted first in mounds about six inches apart—five kernels in a mound. This seemed a terrible waste of seed corn, but Squanto said that people were not the only creatures that needed to eat to sustain life. The birds in the air and the worms in the earth also would need to eat from our garden. So we planted:

Five kernels of corn in a row
One for the blackbird, one for the crow,
One for the cutworm and two to grow.

After the corn sprouted, we planted beans on the sides of the mounds and then squash seedlings between the mounds. Squanto called this a Three Sisters Garden because the three different kinds of plants could support each other, just as the people of our settlement and our Native friends supported each other. The tall corn acted as a pole for the bean vines to climb, and the squash provided a ground cover to hold in moisture and to prevent weeds from overtaking our food crop.

In Europe, we would have fertilized our garden with manure from our farm animals, but we had not brought many animals with us aboard the *Mayflower*. Squanto taught us how to catch herring from the sea and to plant these fish inside the mounds along with the seeds. In this way, the decaying fish could fertilize the Three Sisters seeds.

In the fall, we gathered our harvest and set stores of enough of it in our dwellings to last the coming winter. Our governor then declared that we would rejoice together with our Native friends and give thanks to God for our blessings. My mother and I and three other Pilgrim women cooked the food that we are about to share. We know that our harvest may not always be as plentiful as it is this time, but for today we are grateful for this time of thanksgiving.

My name is Eliza and I am ten years old.

Marilyn Weymouth Seguin
Akron, OH

Author's Note:

One variation of the 'Five Kernels of Corn at Thanksgiving' legend is the annual children's pageant called 'The Corn Planting.' The pageant is held each May at the Harlow Old Fort House Museum in Plymouth, Mass. At the event, the children recite the following rhyme:

Five kernels of corn in a row
One for the blackbird, one for the crow,
One for the cutworm and two to grow.

Sources:

Squanto's Garden by Bill Heid, 2006. Online pdf found at http://nativevillage.org

Jim Baker, 12/14/1998. Comment in blogpost "The Five Kernels of Corn Myth at Thanksgiving."

http://nutfieldgenealogy.blogspot.com, Nov. 28, 2013.

E. M. Barsalou
Dover, NH

Maple Leaves Gather

Down below the hilltop—
Over babbling brook,
Maple leaves gather—
A seasonal ensemble. . .
Of grand wilderness endowments.
Fallen from Spring rains,
As Summer scatters. . .
Floating past mills, leading to pastures,
Engulfing, with their mighty majestic
Tones of gold, yellow, red and amber—
Flowing downstream,
Where still water has collected;
A well-dam may occur and entrap them—
In a yearly gathering.
Below the hilltop, where children once played,
Farm animals carousing—
In the mud, in the hay. . .
In between the seasons grand,
—As so often do,—we too; change
The harvest of crops are resplendent, and gathered soon;
. . .As the maple leaves, gather too—
Beneath an old snowy moon's opulence.

Tamara Kittredge
Vashon Island, WA

It's About a Boy, Wind and Sand

It's about the wind
leaving monuments of it's invisible wrath.
Dunes of silent sand
shaped by the force of the wind's adversity
Sand blown shoreward, delivered,
abandoned now by a collapsed past.
sand collected in shadows and tears
of trees fallen long ago
lying along the windswept shore
of stories whispered, not yet forgotten or forgiven.
It's about a lone boy
sheltered in the dunes
passing the hours, days, weeks
radiant grains of sand warm
against the soles of innocent summer feet
It's about a boy building a monument
to his invincible self.
He is safe in the dunes
outside the paternal wind's reach.

***

Sally Belenardo
Branford, CT

Navy Food

The perfect food for
every sailor to eat is
a navel orange.

Kathleen Guler
Steamboat Springs, CO

Time

Is it true that time speeds faster
As we grow older?
Or is it that I've slowed down
While time rushes past
And I can no longer keep up?

In younger years
Nothing mattered much
Ignore the clock; lots of time yet to explore.
Savor the wisdom in the soaring melody of words,
Of visions, the sunrise, the land's deep, warm breath.

Between years
The clock ruled instead, morning till night
Creativity meant how to get it all done.
Chase money, flee insanity
No time to savor the simplicity of mere thought.

Grown into later years
Steps through the woods falter,
The brilliance of colors fade, and
A long story takes more effort to savor,
As the mind slows a bit more each day.

Where is time going? Is it ever truly lost?
Does it run in circles, waves, patterns?
I need now to relearn patience, go slow,
Once more ignore the clock; to savor wisdom,
The sunrise, the softness of quiet, each day's moments.

Adele Clark D'Alessandro & F. Anthony D'Alessandro
Celebration, FL

Sailing on a Petri Dish

I recently sailed on the ship from hell. My bride and I, nearly octogenarians, planned a Hawaiian cruise several years ago. We scheduled it before Covid-19 blanketed our world. The virus canceled that cruise. Optimistically, we rebooked, at a higher price for a similar cruise to our initial one. We gathered a party of thirteen friends and relatives to join us and traveled to San Francisco to meet our ship in the spring of 2022. Embracing our passports, inoculation records, and our negative Covid-19 test results, we proceeded to what was called the green line at embarkation.

When we arrived at the dock for our sail, my eyes bulged when I was faced with a seemingly never ending snakelike procession of countless passengers in cue for entry to the ship. One hour passed with an advance of what seemed like the baseball distance from home to first base. Seating outside the ship was sparse, and certainly chairs never appeared along the turtle-speed line. Our so-called green line that we worked so hard to attain prior to the cruise, turned into a red stop sign.

Some passengers managed to plop on tiny cement walls while friends and relatives held their spots. At times, despite my nearly four score years, I felt like I possessed the median age on that line. Bottles of water and seats were not an option. In point of fact, the few courteous employees herding us seemed as confused as we were about our entering the ship.

By the third hour, it seemed that some forward progress appeared on the line. We side-stepped aimlessly; however, the entry gate finally appeared. After all the regular tasks required to enter the the boat's bowels ended, we walked on and were greeted by a smiley-faced staff and found our cabin. Unfortunately, our room and tiny refrigerator were

Adele Clark D'Alessandro & F. Anthony D'Alessandro
Celebration, FL

devoid of water even though we had arranged for the full beverage package. We called room service and were advised it would take a while for delivery and so we sought out a dining area and began our food fest.

Slowly, we managed to meet up with our fellow cruisers. Our stress relieved a tad when some of these *cognoscenti* whispered that after the ship's previous cruise had ended, some contracted the virus and those disembarking passengers and cruise workers needed to be extracted for our safety. They whispered that this ship on steroids underwent a thorough decontamination. We finally sailed from the city by the sea with wide grins, toasts, and laughter.

Four long sea days of mingling with both masked and maskless passengers, theater shows, activities, games, exercise, and fine dining followed. After just two days aboard, a few in our group seemed to have contracted what we thought was the common cold. Their symptoms included sneezing, coughing, running noses, and extreme fatigue. Vitamin C and zinc had little healing effect, and so we searched the ship's shops for aspirin and decongestants but to no avail. We then pooled our resources and found some of our friends had had the foresight to bring their own decongestants, aspirin, Tylenol, etc., and we drank all the orange juice available and did the best we could.

Anxiously awaiting our first Hawaiian port of Honolulu, many of us dressed for the occasion donning leis, loud shirts, and beads. In movies, TV, and in travel shows we'd seen all the fanfare and celebration of Hawaiian arrivals. Based on those memories, we fully expected several photographers, bands, dancers, and a Polynesian music fest to greet us. When we docked in Honolulu, my mouth froze and I scratched my head. No one had lined up to welcome us. The dock was barren in terms of festivities. I asked my bride, "Are we in Hawaii, or in a ghost town?"

Some of us lined up for contracted tours from our ship; others hired transport to beaches. Fanfare still failed to exist.

Adele Clark D'Alessandro & F. Anthony D'Alessandro
Celebration, FL

Chatting with our friends and relatives at dinner, we surmised that the next port would open itself to Hawaiian treasures, since we'd yet to see a souvenir store in Honolulu. On the next day Maui would certainly prove different.

Once again, Hawaii failed to deliver the party we expected. As we slowly docked, we were greeted by a sister ship from same cruise line. Passengers from that ship shouted at us from balcony to balcony, "We love you guys!" We speculated, why in the world did we receive such an unusual greeting? Several in our group met and thought that we'd figured it out. Apparently, the internet must have reported stories of our ship carrying Covid-19 patients. Of course, if that were true, our ship was wise to keep it *sub rosa* since it would certainly create panic. We did, however, notice that many more of our casual, maskless passengers began to wear masks in the casino, at meals, at shows, and generally around the ship.

On the buses taking us to sights, more masks donned and a concerto of coughs and sneezes pervaded that closed environment. During our four sightseeing jaunts in Hawaii we visited different unique and historic sites. We were transported in rather luxurious buses from site to site. The common link of my travels was that each bus was stuffed with riders using tissues to rub their noses.

At that point, the first of our sickly group seemed to be feeling better, just as they would with any other cold. Then the next group started their cold-like symptoms. One of the men stayed in his room for two days, while we brought him our pooled medical resources. After a few days, he emerged and joined us again. We started to wonder, "Could this be Covid-19?" No, Covid-19 was a killer, presenting itself with fever, lack of taste buds, and the inability to breathe. Not our symptoms and we let the thought go.

In Oahu we visited a submarine museum but could not arrange to see the *Arizona* because as we were told there were too many of us. My moment on USS *Missouri,* where

Adele Clark D'Alessandro & F. Anthony D'Alessandro
Celebration, FL

General MacArthur had signed surrender documents with Japan, captivated me. After gaping at the ship's enormous guns, I walked in the footsteps of history. I stood in the spot where the peace treaty was inked. My eyes fixed on those documents and sensed that I stood in a live history book initiating goose pimples to attack me.

Another bus took us to Hilo to see jaw dropping falls and outrageous picture book fauna. We were originally scheduled to stop for a luncheon but that was changed to a box lunch. *Why*? That was never explained.

Allow me to reflect on our ship's crowding and spacing situation. As mentioned, our initial boarding line took us almost three hours before stepping onto the ship. We snail-paced back-to-back and head-to-head on a snake-like line.

When cruising, and watching the theater shows, almost every seat was taken, with some standing room only. Every time we visited the casino, it appeared packed with gamblers. When on sanctioned tours and disembarking for ports, we stood on tight long lines. Some passengers wore masks, others did not. When we entered assigned tour buses, every bus we occupied was filled to the brim and we were surrounded by passengers with reams of tissues on their laps.

At the voyage end, we were herded to a crowded exit room and waited another two hours. When we were released to the luggage areas, a swarm of us ran desperately seeking luggage, appearing more hectic than children at a piñata party. Finally, when we entered our approved bus headed to the airport, our driver drove past the domestic terminal, until half the bus shouted simultaneously, "Stop. We get off here!"

Despite our cold symptoms, immediately after getting home we tested for the virus. Both of us proved positive. As the week wore on, we learned that eight of our travel group of thirteen had contracted the virus. We looked at each other and my bride said, "I felt that we were part of an experiment and never warned about the Covid-19 situation. Tony, it seems like we sailed on a gigantic Petri Dish."

Mary Ann Bedwell
Grants, NM

Vultures Rest on the Cottonwood Trees

Vultures perch on the bone-white branches
of the desert cottonwood in my neighbor's yard,
waiting for the breath of the desert wind.

Tipping from side to side,
they clutch and release their talons,
flap and refold their wings.
One or two lift off, settle back on their limb.

As I watch, a few decide the time has come and
launch themselves into the sky,
arching their wings to take the best advantage
of the early rush of air.

Soon the air is full, the V's of their wings act like
boomerangs
as they cross and recross the sky.
Some spiral upward, passing out of sight,
reappearing as they descend.

Eventually, all will return,
waiting for the next opportunity
to fly.

Karen E. Wagner
Hudson, MA

Paddling Still Water

for my brother

I'll show you where you
can paddle that canoe.
Wood Ducks move through
the early mist as it rises.
Loons laze, throw
their crazed calls we hear at sunset.
She and I meet near rivers like this too.
Is this your aspiration?

There's a planet I often see
on the horizon, known for her beauty.
Venus hovers,
just above her reflection
in glassed waters
where I have her permission to show you too.
Paint that into your thoughts.
Sharp, radiant, as distinctive
as a full moon.

I can't hold this for you indefinitely.
I've told you many times that hiking
and snowshoeing are excellent here.
Each season brings and takes
as it will. If it's September there'll be
loosestrife. Loons winter
off the coast. Ducks fly south
in early autumn. For the sake
of generations, spring chicks cluster
in the cold shoreline waters.

Karen E. Wagner
Hudson, MA

Remember that hooded fur jacket
we had? You wore it like bearskin,
crawled around growling,
and pawed for a den.

A river like this runs close by.
Loon wails waft through chilled air.

***

Sister Irene Zimmerman
Greenfield, WI

Late-August Rain

A rumble of thunder woke me during the night.
A loud sigh of cool wind riffled the shriveled leaves
and tassels of parched corn, sending a message
to its roots: *Rain's coming*!
The rain tiptoed, then raced across the fields.
Corn stalks guzzled their fill in the dark.
Thirsty soybeans, having withstood the heat
better than the corn, lifted yellowed leaves.

On the porch, Dave's dogs howled
as thunder crashed against their ear drums.
The screen door squeaked when Dave stepped out.
Quiet down, you lucky puppies, I heard him say,
This million-dollar rain's gonna buy sausage
for you every week all next winter.

Reyann Brooks
Gorham, ME

Self-portrait with Corvus

I call out but you don't answer,
Too busy preening your new feathers that she purchased
for you.
I fell under your pinning spell, craved the ever-changing
color of your eyes—
Dark blue, violet, dark blue.
My perfected song eventually wasn't good enough.
Do you still remember how easily I seduced you?
She doesn't have that power.
Underneath gilded talons with their gaudy rings, she's
hollow.
Hollow like these bones that wither each day she taunts
you, hollow like my voice that was
once alluring.
Look what you've done; I've turned black, my song is no
longer attractive.
I sing with a rasp.
When I'm done, you'll be drenched in red, and I'll watch her
strip your body of those colorful
feathers.
You left me with a boring call, a simple design...
But don't underestimate the power of a murder.

Victoria Rose
Fletcher, NC

Capturing a Moment

The oversized envelope slipped through the pile of mail. The large handwritten address provoked my curiosity, along with the absence of a return address. Most of the mail was for continuing education programs and advertisements. Tired from a long day, I was not sure I wanted to find out, right now, what this uninvited envelope held. After pouring a glass of water and putting some leftovers in the microwave, I picked up the envelope. There was no indication of its content. I sighed and opened it. One item emerged, a black-and-white photo, of one person.

Time continued while my memory froze. As the familiarity began to seep in, I turned the photograph over and found three handwritten words. “Please call me.” The number to call was written in clear, large numbers, similar to the large letters of the plea. I again turned to the picture, searching for something. Trying to recognize the person that at one time was the most familiar person in my life.

This was not the first, or second, request. After all, for ten years I avoided seeing her. Nothing could change my opinion of what she did. Even hearing, through an extensive network, that she was ill, I refused to alter how I felt.

This time, the face in the picture haunted me. The young woman in the picture had more freckles. Thick hair lay along the ground haphazardly, showing no gray. The shirt was nondescript and was probably purchased in a rack of other simple shirts marked reduced. The scoop neckline revealed a wooden necklace in the shape of a heart. Deep, alluring, surrounded by full eyebrows, her eyes were easily the center of the photo. Lips expressing a slight playfulness framed her mouth. There was a natural reaction to turn the picture, so she would appear to be standing, but she was horizontal, possibly resting her back on steps or a stone. In the background spots of sun and shade scattered beyond her body. There were no recognizable features to indicate where it was taken. But that was the simplest of mysteries I wanted to uncover. I wanted to know who this person was, and what happened to her.

The eyes I remembered were rarely playful. Most of the time, they were weary, defensive, expecting something to go wrong. Her voice tended to be unsure, anticipating the next problem. Her language and eyes didn't match. Her words were encouraging and thoughtful. In the later years of her marriage to my father, her voice and language became more forceful, more commanding. I resented that so much. At night, hearing them argue, her strong voice kept me up long after the argument was over. But then, the argument was never over. I was reminded often of her resistance to let it go. My father, her husband, for days condemning her refusal to let the argument go.

My curiosity responded to the request, and after a few weeks my body yielded. I pulled into the hospital parking lot, remembering the fighting and chaos, feeling the tension it created. I questioned why I came, taking time out of my busy schedule to see someone who made a choice to leave. Maybe I just wanted to finally let it go, to stop being haunted by the loss. I thought about just entering the room, telling her to go to hell, and walking out. She didn't deserve much more than that. Then I caught hold of my anger, choosing instead to act dignified. To accomplish that, I put up my emotional shield.

She was sitting up, reading a book, when I walked in. I don't know exactly what I expected, but I didn't think I expected her to look so healthy. She must have noticed the look in my eyes and said "I'm not on my deathbed. I'm just in for some treatments. I'm not going away that easily."

I don't know how she meant that. I had been trying to get her out of my mind for a long time now. Not due to death, simply from an understanding that what she had done meant she lost my respect, giving me no reason to want to be

Victoria Rose
Fletcher, NC

with her.

"I know you are still mad at me. Can I ask, what persuaded you to call me?"

I couldn't find my voice, so I just held up the envelope.

"I had hoped that would pique your curiosity," she said, softly, in a voice I barely recognized.

My eyes rested on the book on her lap, and she answered my question without my having to ask. "It's good, has a lot of research, and breaks through layers of illusions about things we've taken as gospel truth."

"I am so very glad you came. I have missed you every single day, since..." and her voice trailed off, the way people lose the ability to say that someone died.

The anger in me quickly rose, and I responded with its force, "So, why did you leave then?"

She didn't answer my question. She closed her eyes and remained still. Finally, she looked at me and asked me what I thought of the picture she sent. I took it out of the envelope and held it up for her. "This one?" I asked, testing to see if my voice would cooperate.

"Yes, that one"

"I hardly recognized you."

"I didn't recognize myself, when I first saw it, some twenty years after it was taken. By that time, the person in the picture was so hidden I had forgotten her completely. What a gift, to have it sent to me," she said as though dreaming of another life.

"Did *he* take the picture?" Again, she didn't answer.

"Oh, child, we'll get to that. I have plenty of time to get to that."

We sat in silence for a while. I wasn't sure if she was physically, or emotionally tired. She broke the silence, "People often commented about my eyes. It was so uncomfortable. They would look at me, right into my eyes. I would avoid their eyes at all cost. I'd look at the ground, at my shoes, and if I was lucky, they were holding something, then

Victoria Rose
Fletcher, NC

I could comment about it, and we would both be able to look at something, anything, but focus on my eyes."

"That makes no sense. If people liked your eyes, why did you hate the attention?" I could hear the anger in my voice.

"All I wanted was to be seen for who I was, not for what I looked like. I was born with my eyes, no choice was involved. When people focused on my eyes I felt as though everything else about me was overlooked, if not ignored altogether."

She took a sip of water from the plastic hospital cup. She didn't appear to expect a response, and I was unwilling to comment on what I saw in her.

"You probably don't remember your grandparents, do you?" she asked.

"No"

"When they first met your father, they were mortified. 'What do you see in that reckless, sorry excuse of a man?' " they asked.

"What did Dad say?"

"We just laughed and laughed and laughed."

"Until...you stopped laughing." I reminded her.

"Until the laughter stopped."

I moved to the window, watching people come and go, some with balloons, some with tears. How odd, to have birth and death in one building.

"That picture was taken before I knew your dad. People say a picture captures a moment. There were so many things not captured in this picture, things I am still trying to recover. What I did feel, for the first time ever, was the beauty of this person, the simplicity and the ease of her."

I pulled myself away from the trance of the picture, and faced my mother, no longer holding back my anger. "Is that why you wanted to see me? So you could try and explain who you are to me? As if you haven't shown me?"

Her eyes looked into mine, absent any fear, anger, or sadness. She just looked at me, completely. "I wanted you to come, so you could be more aware of who you are."

Victoria Rose
Fletcher, NC

"What gives you that right?" I demanded.

"It's not my right. It's my obligation, as just one of your ancestors."

Our eyes locked, in defiance, infinitely intertwined. I felt I would shatter into minuscule particles if I looked away, yet the uncomfortable tension continued to build. As though on cue, a nurse came in. I appreciated the opportunity to break the visual connection. The nurse silently took my mother's temperature, blood pressure, and checked the IV. Once out of the room, my mother spoke again.

"I was with my father when he died." I don't know where the words came from. I simply heard myself say, "I'm sorry I was never good enough."

She closed her eyes, and I could see her muscles tense, and then slowly release. When she opened her eyes, they were distant, lost in another time and place. This time, when our eyes met, they recognized a familiarity that we both wanted to avoid. My skin felt clammy, my stomach nauseous. With unfamiliar tenderness, my mother said, "That picture was taken fifteen years before your grandfather died, three years before I married your father. That picture was taken in a small window of time when I had the courage to discover and feel who I was."

"Did your boyfriend take the picture?"

She nodded yes.

"Were you faithful to him?"

"No, but not in the way you mean. I didn't fool around or cheat on him. I just didn't know who to be or feel without the doubts, fears, or believing I was not worthy. I wasn't faithful to myself. I reverted into someone unsure, defensive."

"So you made a choice to be unhappy and afraid?"

"It's not that black and white. For just a short time, I left what I was familiar with, and experienced what it was like to be respected and appreciated."

"If you're going to blame your mistakes on your parents, then be ready to accept the consequences of my mistakes."

My words surprised me.

"I stopped blaming them years ago. I've had to accept the responsibility and consequences for my choices."

I moved from the window momentarily. Faced with the drab hospital room, faded pictures, white sheet, plastic cup, and pitcher, I chose to turn again to gaze out the window. I caught my reflection in the glass, and for a brief second, questioned how much I knew myself. I brushed the thought away.

"What is so respectful about having an affair?" The force of my anger was so consistent it felt normal.

"Yes, it's time to fill in some of the gaps. Watching you grow up I realized how important it was to stop the familiar pattern of being small and unworthy. As I began to take on more responsibility for myself, I began to reject the blame that was directed at me. I began to be aware, of myself, of my worth. That caused a lot of friction between your dad and me. He tried. I tried. I wanted the marriage to survive. No matter what I did or said I was not strong enough to be seen for who I was, or at least, the person I kept trying to be."

She stopped to refresh her throat. I knew if I turned slightly, I'd see her reflection in the glass, but I chose to look at the strangers coming and going.

"I don't have to tell you how difficult it was. You lived through it, the fighting and tension. The more I tried to set boundaries, to be respected, the fighting intensified. You don't need to know all the details, and you already know firsthand what the experience was like. Anyway, I reached a point where I just wanted nothing to do with men. That in itself was so unusual for me since growing up I was a tomboy and found it easier to relate to boys. I think what I hated most about puberty was losing those uncomplicated friendships. Suddenly, there was this sexual aspect to them, but that's all another story or a diversion."

She took another break, and I began to realize how thirsty I was. I was adamant about keeping a distance, so ignored my body's need.

"There was so much going on for me at that time, as your dad and I tried and tried, and failed and failed. There was so much sadness, exhaustion, and frustration. I reached a point where I really, really missed being appreciated. All I wanted was someone, a man specifically, to look into my eyes and honestly, passionately, say 'I appreciate you for all you do.' I kept hoping that it would be your dad, but hope was no longer possible. I wanted to hear those words without any strings attached, anger, control, or resentment. All the harmful behavior I was trying so desperately to remove from my relationship with your dad."

"Poor victim," I said.

"I am well aware that it takes two, and I realize I was part of the problem. In case you haven't noticed, I've paid the consequences for my faults."

There was an edge in her voice, and it echoed in the silence. I turned to look at her, propped up by the pillows. I hardly recognized her somewhat pale, thin body.

"Are you sure you want to hear this?" She asked the same way she used to ask after explaining the danger of a choice I was about to make.

"Out of the blue, this photo was sent to me. I cried, with grief, wondering where that wild spirit went all these years. I corresponded for a while with my former boyfriend. I was reminded of how easy it had been to laugh, talk, and dream. Once my dreams returned, I knew I needed to do the hardest thing I'd ever done. Not because of, or for, someone else. For me. For my heart."

My mind began to spin with confusion. It didn't match up. I came to tell her to go to hell, and now I didn't know what to think.

Gently, her voice drifted through my confusion. "Remember how I used to tell you that if you can't find a solution, try asking a different question? After all these years, did you ever ask what I wrote in my journal, or, what

Victoria Rose
Fletcher, NC

your father was doing reading it?"

"I don't need to ask any other question than how could you leave?"

"Now who sounds like a victim?"

"What do you call someone whose mother ran away from her family for another man? You weren't there when I needed you, so I learned not to need you."

"Have you asked whether you were there for me when I needed you?"

"You are the parent, the adult. You're supposed to be there for me."

"I called you three to four times a week, but you refused to talk to me. I wrote you letters. I invited you to every event I thought might interest you. When I was informed of your activities, I was rarely informed, I attended. Included with the invitations I sent to you I let you know we could do things differently, we could choose to do what we wanted to do. In every way possible, you distanced yourself from me. So, now, explain to me, who was not there?" The words were spoken, slowly, purposefully. I didn't want to believe her. There was no way she could know how hurt I had been.

The silence swallowed us up. My mind envisioned that night, as clear as the red exit light. I recalled her face, so worn and in shock as my father yelled angrily, "Are you having an affair." The scene was etched in my memory. The house shrank as she stood firm, refusing to defend her dignity by answering his accusations. I believed the only one left, my father, as he yelled after her, "You must be guilty if you don't answer!" Hate filled me as my eyes watched her back. It was so vivid, even after all these years. This time some of the gaps became visible. Why didn't I remember him saying he wanted to know because his marriage was falling apart? Or her shock that he had read her diary. Did she really respond by stating, "So, rely on the same thing that hasn't worked, find a way to blame me!" She disappeared in the cold winter night, leaving him holding her empty coat as she fled

Victoria Rose
Fletcher, NC

into a darkness that offered no shadows. All I could hear now was the static of the exit light until her voice found its way to me.

"You were so young, really. Unfortunately, you witnessed more than someone at sixteen should witness. Maybe this will help."

She held out an oversized envelope. I sighed, opened it, and saw the eyes, joy, and playfulness of someone I hardly recognized. Someone I vaguely remembered as playful, curious. Someone I had locked away ten years ago. I looked into my mother's eyes, unsure of how to let go.

Softly, the sound entered my body. "What do you want, now?"

***

Kate Kearns
Scarborough, ME

Miracle Bench

The one by the ferry station
where passers wait their ships,
where shadow branches
imperfect the granite cobbles,
where generations of cigarettes
have burned through their lives,
where four oaks have been spared
a square of soil each,
where voices know each other's names
but not my name, and where,
if you sit long enough,
a car's open window will
gift the four corners with Beyoncé.

Jean Biegun
Davis, CA

Spring on Marsh Trail

Hawk regal on bush
wrens align in late spring snow
motionless, waiting

Morning blackbird shriek
bark of one lone startled fawn
our boots too heavy

Pastel breeze flutters
blossoms lift to coral skies
blue wings flicker near

Kingfisher plummets
alder pollen dances free
this moment, fleet moment

Water strider skates
on the sun's white reflection
cars pass on 310

Red dogwood at night
glistens in black slanting rain
when lightning flares near

Marsh trail in full moon
woodcock leaps unseen but heard
our times here, perfect

Robert B. Moreland
Pleasant Prairie, WI

Lucifer

for the people of Ukraine. Never give up. Never surrender.

The lie that denies itself holding tight
to the perception built on shifting sand
that human life is sacred, that any evil
is okay in one's own moral judgement.

Truth is relative, there are no absolutes
except maybe vodka. Rewrite history?
No problem. Stalin did it. There is precedent.
No disagreement or one may wake up dead.

Nuclear blackmail is the furnace that
reveals the cowardice of the world.
Nations tremble in the specter of the flash,
verdant world becomes a doomed cinder.

But that is on those who continue to feed
the lie, allow the carnage, make up history.
If repeated long enough the lie becomes truth
erasing anything that had gone before.

Lucifer perceived he was superior to God.
Pride lives the lie that everything is fine,
rearrange the deck chairs on the *Titanic*,
and relish that long plummet to a fiery hell.

Julie Babb
Damariscotta, ME

To Vincent—Wherever You May Be...

For so many years now
I have watched the stars
As they enter the sky, shyly at first,
Gaining their strength as
The night's dusk returns.
They sparkle like children's eyes
On Christmas morning
Or the early snow
That cloaks my small garden
With\diamonds.

When I was a child I imagined
That I could hear the stars
Singing to their universe and,
Somehow, singing just to me...
Now I have grown old enough to hear
Their truth—they sing not just to me
But to all who, with reverent breath
Held in wonder, listen knowing
It is the very song of our creation.

Van Gogh, in his loneliness,
Knew the notes, the song so well—
He sang it in swirls of stardust and paint
He cried out "Listen! Listen!"
In his colors of cloud and sky—
He saw the voyages of the stars

Peggy Faye Brown
Gray, ME

The Case for Preserving Books

One of my favorite joys is to be at the ocean. My senses compile the smell of crisp air, the sounds of crashing waves and squawking gulls, the sensation of warm and textured sand, and of course, the beautiful scenery. Exploring and discovering a keepsake shell concludes the day. My windowsills overflow with these souvenirs.

Problems of the world made it difficult to travel over the past few summers. I missed taking walks at Mackworth Island, Scarborough Beach, and Chebeague Island. I missed the ferry rides in Casco Bay. My annual day trip to a special area on the Blue Hill peninsula didn't happen either out of respect for the health and safety of residents.

In my quest to be near water, I visited Rockport, but not by driving. I pulled *A Seal Called Andre*, by Harry Goodridge and Lew Dietz, from my bookshelf and blew off the dust. I settled in and truly enjoyed this story. I've had the book for years but never read it. I still recall hearing my parents say, "Andre's home," while reading the *Bangor Daily News* during my childhood in Hampden, Maine. The book isn't just about Andre; it recalls a different pace of life experienced by Mainers in the 60's and 70's.

It dawned on me that during that era, my family tended to sort of "shelter in place" when not at work or school. We stayed home. We explored our woods and yard, rode bikes, worked around the house, and cooked at home. We sewed, made crafts, wrote, and read. Since I had a little free time the other day, I even rediscovered one of my favorite childhood backyard adventures; looking up and watching the clouds form shapes as they swirl around against the beautiful blue sky. I let my mind relax and enjoy the show. The canvas in the sky was sprinkled with my imagination as I observed dragons, whales, and even a seal like Andre float overhead.

Peggy Faye Brown
Gray, ME

When I returned Andre's book to my bookcase, I noticed *The Edge of the Sea* by Rachel Carson was gathering dust also. With the beautiful illustrations by Bob Hines, this book is a true joy. Rachel discusses the life forms at the shore and what they do. Always thinking barnacles did nothing but cut my feet when stepped on, Rachel's notations inspired me to learn more about them. Did you know larvae glue their heads to rocks before creating their shelled adult forms? Fascinating!

While always grateful to be a Mainer, I am also grateful for the Mainers who shared their stories of Maine's seashore and gave me a new perspective by which to enjoy them while at home. These books endure and teach, even when a trip to the water isn't feasible. I look forward to ocean visits this summer.

Fortunately, traveling has become an option again. On a recent trip to the New York Public Library, I was delighted to find Rachel Carson's typed manuscript of *Silent Spring* on display. This was also on my home bookshelf, but I had not yet read it. Upon my return home, I researched more about this very significant book. I learned she reached out to E.B. White while he worked for the *New Yorker*, hoping he would observe a court hearing on insecticides.

Letters of E. B. White also lives in my bookcase. I flipped the pages and sure enough, a letter referencing Rachel Carson's work is there. A few months later, I received Margaret Atwood's *Burning Questions* as a gift. What did I find inside? Two essays about Rachel Carson.

Depth is added to knowledge when authors, books, and topics intersect. Discovering these twists and turns is like taking a Sunday drive on country roads while exploring Maine. You just might discover your new favorite place to visit.

Journeys inside my bookcase took me back to the past, into the future, and around the world. I learned about barnacles with Rachel Carson and joyous friend reunions with

Peggy Faye Brown
Gray, ME

Andre the Seal. I also learned about whale hunting missions with Herman Melville and was reminded of adolescence with Judy Blume. I leaped into the inquisitive minds of E.B. White and Margaret Atwood, and obtained guidance and advice from Maya Angelou and Alex Trebek.

Recently, I decided to take a journey outside my bookcase. I wanted warm chocolate chip cookies for a quick and chilly springtime trip to the ocean. As I lined the baking sheet with parchment paper and turned the oven dial, I was suddenly reminded how 451 is the temperature at which paper burns. This fact has remained with me for over 40 years from the time I read Ray Bradbury's impactful novel in high school and why preserving my books is critical. When the cookies were done, I pulled *Fahrenheit 451* from my bookshelf to take with me. I will never stop appreciating the ocean, books, or authors.

***

Cordula Mathias
Trevett, ME

Summer Song

Water, soft and cool
offers its liquid embrace.

Stroke after stroke
the lake works healing magic
on skin raw from stress.

Percussive noise of
an over-heated brain
segues into rippling melody.

Bunny L. Richards
Trescott Twp., ME

Leaving Early

Wind pulls hackmatack branches
golden needles thrown
willy-nilly as
maple leaves curled like
crippled mice dance
across the road,
fetch up on withered hardhack.

Gulls circle sheltered coves
mournful cries lost
in Sunday's push and pull.
Deserted urchins
gutted into brittle bowls
adorn lichen splashed rocks
beyond the gated entrance.

On farther shore, where slackened
tide leaves pebbled beach
Annie drunk, confused, half-dressed
abandoned to cold night, stumbles
then falls into permanent sleep.

Marjorie Arnett
Belfast, ME

Final Gig

Tufts of grey hair sprout
from under the old ball cap
and from the arms of his
frayed flannel shirt calloused
hands appear. When he talks,
his fists hit the table as if for the
past twenty years no one listened.
She is jutting knees and tall,
more overgrown boy than girl,
her gender not clear until
she said what she said to the man.
It's Annie, Grandpa. It's time.
He moves slowly from behind
the table as if his foot has gone
to sleep. I can do this Annie.
He waves his hand in the air,
his course bawdy voice filled
with indignation. Yellow squares
of light lie on the floor of the old
grange hall. He hobbles toward
the stage, fiddle tucked under his arm.

P. C. Moorehead
North Lake, WI

The Flowing Stream

A stream from its source
in mountains far, reaches sand
and sinks into marsh.

The stream's voice echoes
through mire and the misty fog.
"Let me be again."

"Let me run freely
on a cleaner, fresher path.
Let me be better."

Life hears and answers:
"Dear stream, you want a new choice?
Of course, run anew."

"Run life's way in joy.
Share your gifts; do what's right.
We applaud your good fight."

John T. Hagan
Springboro, OH

Kelly's Field

Quite likely, many of those coming of age in the United States during the twentieth century had or experienced a childhood or early teenaged haunt where impromptu competitions or games, forbidden topics, world mysteries, and personal triumphs (or firsts) were played, discussed, imagined, or exaggerated. It was that hallowed part of the neighborhood where a gang as few as three or as many as fifteen assembled in "flash mobs" long before those buzzwords were coined. It was also largely a time before video games, internet, smartphones, social media, and all manner of technological innovations replaced the in-person interactions and dynamics that were the staples of American life.

For this writer, that treasured place was known as Kelly's Field, so named for Mrs. Kelly, the rarely seen dowager who lived in an enormous (by our standards) gray and stately home on a 3 or 4-acre property that included a detached 4 or 5-space garage under a flat, concrete, balcony-type roof of variable uses. Next to the house and garage a rather steep and lengthy asphalt driveway ran down to my quiet street. Adjacent to the structures and driveway were approximately three acres of open space, dappled here and there by gnarly crabapple trees.

Rather oddly, the property was bordered on three sides by Rugby Road, Norman Avenue, and Catalpa Drive, sparsely trafficked streets characterized by lowly-to-modestly-priced homes built in the 1920's, 30's, or 40's when the area was largely farmland. I and my two older brothers and parents lived in a two-bedroom bungalow on Rugby about a half-block from Kelly's, just far enough away that I could claim ignorance to my mother's high-pitched summons from our front screen door at ten o'clock on summer nights.

For us "Rugby Roaders," as we largely thought of our-

John T. Hagan
Springboro, OH

selves, the typical approach to Kelly's Field was made from Rugby, on which most of my neighborhood friends lived as well. As such, our bicycles would navigate almost on autopilot to Kelly's and be "parked" (sometimes with kickstand but mostly thrown down haphazardly) in the asphalt driveway on just about any spring, summer, or early fall day when the strictures of school days were not in force.

The range of confabs, competitions, games, or skullduggery was broad, and depending upon the season or month, they might be multifaceted. Among the more prominent uses of this stronghold were our spring and summer softball games that had protocols peculiar to Kelly's Field. Since the acreage next to the house and garage had not depth enough to protect windows on Norman Avenue from spheroids of baseball size, softball was the sport of choice (which is not to suggest that a well-hit Rawlings from one of the older players never resulted in the sickening sound of shattering glass, followed by an expedient and wholesale exodus of the multitude). Furthermore, the usable space was less than half the open acres, as one side was a sharply sloped expanse that ran down to Catalpa Drive.

Owing to the limitations of participants, our softball games would generally number no more than six or seven on a side, with the pitcher and catcher routinely fielding for both teams (and the pitcher serving as umpire whose authority was invariably impeachable). Ball gloves were often shared, as some did not own one or had left it at home. Prudent competitors kept their gloves in near perpetuity on the handlebars of their bikes. Since right field was in the declivity, it was by topography and tradition an automatic out. Choosing sides was generally left to two of the older or more talented players, and they were quite judicious in their selections and with a ruthless disregard for the feelings of those chosen last (as participation-trophy egalitarianism had yet to be conceived). One ritual, as religiously observed as the National Anthem before high school, college, and profession-

John T. Hagan
Springboro, OH

al sporting events, was the ceremonial anointment of the team to bat first. This iconic preamble was enacted by the two captains who would take the marred and pocked Louisville Slugger in their hands and alternatingly climb the ball bat grip-by-grip until the winner grasped the last available space with no "chicken grips" allowed.

Among the typically assembled ball players were two or three girls who became decreasingly tomboyish over the years and who would blossom into fetching teenagers at the nearby public high school. One, however, could hold her own in any footrace, ballgame, or competition with nearly every boy. I will call her Donna because that was her name. She could run the bases, hit the ball, and field the grounders and flies as well as anyone, and she was invariably among the first to be chosen for a team. Donna was a raven-haired, brown-eyed Italian whose short shorts and sleeveless T-shirts in the summer exposed naturally tanned gams and arms that were becoming more of a distraction each year.

Kelly's Field was also perfectly suited for games like kick-the-can, gang tag, or flashlight tag, owing to its myriad places to escape or hide. The unlocked garage ports provided hasty refuges, and the window wells of the cavernous house were perfect "foxholes" to avoid the beam of a flashlight or the night vision of a pursuer. Of enduring delight for me was the night I found myself in one of the window wells with Donna, who was becoming less a fellow street runner while besotting me with first love. When she urged me to "wait a few more minutes" before we broke with catlike speed to kick the can in a game of that name, she seared a memory in me that traverses the years and distances to that long ago time and place. I sometimes wonder if like Boo Radley in *To Kill a Mockingbird,* Mrs. Kelly was watching us wistfully and yearning for her own carefree youth. In those halcyon years of our activities on her property, she never once scolded or rebuked us for making too much commotion or noise.

Autumn months gave rise to two-hand touch football

games among the boys at Kelly's Field, and they were never without arguments over whether the actual touch was made, the receiver was in-bounds, or the runner was over the goal line (marked by the knobby trunk of a crabapple tree). Such disputes might be settled by peacemakers or result in a premature end to the game in which boredom had already encroached or rain had dampened a zeal for victory.

Winter days accompanied by snow would find us using Mrs. Kelly's steep driveway on Flexible Flyers to sled down to Rugby Road where a lookout had been commissioned to watch for cars. Our sleds were those used for years before by older siblings or neighborhood kids, and these wood-steel transports could carry as many as three at a time piled on to one another. The trick, mastered only by seasoned drivers, was to "hit the brakes" (shoe tips grinding in snow) before crashing into the curb on the opposite side of Rugby. Helmets, mouth guards, and other safety gear were accoutrements not even imagined by the Kelly's Field daredevils of our day; and loose teeth, fat lips, or bloody noses were not rare. The more the snow packed, the faster the run, and we remained until fingers and toes surrendered to the freezing temps or the cravings of empty bellies exceeded the exhilaration of our madcap dashes to the street.

As previously mentioned, Kelly's Field provided a multiplicity of purposes and experiences. The concrete expanse that served as the roof of the huge garage actually began at ground level in the house's side yard and extended out over the four or five ports below. For safety reasons, it had an iron railing around it with an opening on the yard side to access its use. In the mansion's heyday, it may have served as a gathering place for summer soirees or autumn costume parties. Each corner of the railing had a mounted sconce to accommodate an illumination of some kind.

To this elevation the interlopers would often gravitate after dark in the summer to regale each other with the latest gossip or to pontificate upon world or local matters pro-

John T. Hagan
Springboro, OH

foundly beyond their ken. Nothing was more intriguing to these *ad hoc* assemblies than some "inside" or lurid information about an accident, scandal, or breakup. Among the intelligences shared at night were revelations such as what caused babies, which was for me at aged ten the closest I would come to a birds-and-bees session with my dad. This earth-shaking enlightenment was bestowed upon me by Norman, a three-years-my-senior man-of-the-world. I will rationalize my naivete as caused by my K–12 parochial school attendance, while living in a neighborhood populated almost entirely of public school students. In retrospect, I suspect that many fathers in mid-to-late twentieth century America relied upon such street education to relieve them of any seat-shifting discussions about life.

The garage balcony after dark also afforded some of life's inaugurals, such as my first kiss, which I received in seventh grade from a girl I will call Janice. Although Janice was not my heartthrob, as Donna was, she jettisoned me into a new experience that would not replicate for me until my senior prom. Talk about your late bloomer!

While Kelly's Field is the stuff of nostalgia for me, it is likely no more special than the ubiquitous hangouts for the youthful gatherings of countless others, and certainly no more revered.

Elizabeth Lombardo
Walpole, ME

The Longing

You don't know how ardently I longed for you,
how impatiently I waited,
as winter veiled all hope and desire.
How I disdained spring's beauty
when at last the veil was drawn
and her fullness surpassed my own.
Each tender new bud,
every leaf that unfurled with the blush of green youth
seemed to mock the dark caverns
where soft sunlight could not reach.
Do you know the jealousy I felt toward each bird coupled merrily in its nest?
Every fallow field turned over in anticipation of the seed?
Earth's heart pounded in vigor around me
while mine lay cold among old leaves.
Wishing to share in the fledgling's pure delight,
to find abandon in heights of clearest skies,
exhaling the fears of winter's famine
and suffusing the soul with the warmth of promise.
Stiff with frost, my heart still waits, grounded and unthawing.
Yet though I cannot lift my voice with the gentle breeze,
the song of life's renewal reverberates from above
proclaiming hope lies dormant, but never dead.
And so I trust, with every sleeping root, my companion,
that I, too, will spring forth to embrace the new light.

Kathy Ott-McHugh
Kennebunk, ME

Highchair 1985

dedicated to my son Jason

If you want you can sit
In the highchair one last time
Before I give it away.
You can slip under the tray.
And I'll remember your red jello fingers,
Flattened chocolate cake crumbs and
Streams of milk underneath your elbows.
The rocking of your body, back and forth.
The thumping of your feet, one at a time.
Where you could sit for an hour investigating gravity.
And though you probably would still sit
I watch you climb onto a kitchen chair.
The highchair is in your way
And I move it out of the way.
I have grown a little myself today.

***

John Gillespie
Camden, ME

the answer

the answer, whatever that was,
came during the night.

in the morning, all we could see
was some chicken tracks in the dooryard

nothing more was given,
and nothing said.

Hans Krichels
Bucksport, ME

My Phlebotomist

At the clinic this morning,
getting checked out for borderline anemia...
(we grow old, we grow old...)
I told my phlebotomist—Janet, she told me to call her—
I told her that phlebotomists of yore had had trouble
finding veins in my arm.
Janet smiled knowingly and told me about her father,
who'd had veins bulging like hawsers,
and a young trainee one time who'd stabbed and stabbed
and prepared to stab some more...
Until her father had grabbed the needle and
completed the procedure without her.
Janet grinned at the thought.
But, not you, she said; *you're what we call a hard stick.*
I rolled up my sleeve,
and Janet told me about her own difficulties
following her breast cancer and chemotherapy;
certain veins, she told me were off limits
for the needle-bearers; others were hard to find.
We're a pair of turnips, she confided;
It's hard to get blood out of us.
She eyed and poked at my inner elbow
with the touch of an angel and the vision of an eagle.
A single easy stick, and the job was completed.
I rolled down my sleeve and went home
With new appreciation for phlebotomists in general—
not to mention the turnips growing in my garden.

Juliana L'Heureux
Topsham, ME

A Time Traveler Monument

If a phenomenon like time traveling exists on planet Earth, then the Vietnam Wall Memorial in Washington, DC is one place where it happens. Walking the pathway, beginning at the center and solemnly strolling through the reflective granite, while touring the length of the famous wall, is a tribute to honor those who lost their lives fighting in the Vietnamese jungles.

Walking slowly, while meditating on the inscribed names, is a time traveling immersion into the past lives of 58,000 young people who died in Vietnam during a vain attempt to defeat the northern communist National Liberation People's Army created by Ho Chi Minh.

Located on the National Mall in Washington, DC, the stunning black granite memorial is located north of the Lincoln Memorial and the Reflecting Pool.

American men and women who served and died in the Vietnam War (1959–1975) are memorialized; each one by their name inscribed on the wall. The memorial consists of three parts: the Vietnam Veterans Memorial Wall, the Three Servicemen Statue and Flagpole, and the Vietnam Women's Memorial. By the grace of God, my husband is not one of the names on the wall.

Frankly, I had little interest to visit this amazing memorial when it was unveiled on the National Mall and Memorial Parks. My husband, Richard, was deployed twice to Vietnam while we were a U.S. Navy family. He served in Chu Lai with the Navy Seabees, stationed with the Marines and then again aboard the U.S.S. *Intrepid*, "the Fighting I," CVS11, in the Gulf of Tonkin. In fact, the Seabee base at Chu Lai was under attack nearly every day when he was there, because the mission within the base was to build airfields. The Marines provided security for the Seabees as they construct-

Juliana L'Heureux
Topsham, ME

ed the airbase.

Our family's Vietnam experiences did not end with my husband's two deployments.

As fate would have it, my family was with my husband when we were stationed in Subic Bay, in the Philippines on April 30, 1975, the day when Vietnam fell to the communist forces.

Newsreels showing the chaos and mass exodus of refugees trying to escape their government's collapse by climbing onto helicopters hovered over the U.S. embassy in Saigon, were the same people who were received by the thousands into U.S. Philippine military bases located in Subic, Cubi, and Clark Air Force Base.

Why would I want to visit the Vietnam War Memorial? Like reliving a bad dream, it seemed to me, there was no reason to meditate on a stone monument when my desire was to suppress the entire era and my family's difficult experiences. Nevertheless, when my husband was given a temporary Navy duty assignment to attend a college program at American University, the weekends were free and ideal for tourism. Although visiting the Vietnam Memorial was the last place on my list of places to visit in monument rich Washington, DC, we finally decided to pack up a stroller and our two young sons to make a very brief excursion there, if only to say we did.

But, we were drawn like time travelers into the names. About two hour later, after we walked the entire length of the wall, we were moved to tears and found ourselves not wanting to leave.

Visitors are drawn into the time travel memorial because we witness the reflection of ourselves while reading the thousands of names carved in the shiny black stone. We saw our faces reading the names of young people who actually lived at one time. They become like ghosts in our reflections. We touched some of the names. We mourned with those who placed red roses beneath their relatives' names and who are

Juliana L'Heureux
Topsham, ME

honored in the stone. We watched our reflections while thinking about the names of those who could still be alive. But, the names are those who were sent to fight in a foreign war where the North Vietnamese enemy army and the allies in South Vietnam all looked alike. American fighters were in harm's way just by virtue of their size and being of different ethnicities. Americans were unable to hide in the reeds along the banks of the Mekong River. No average-sized American could fit into a hole to slide underground and hide in the jungle in the Cu Chi Tunnels.

As time passed, my husband and I came to suppress our feelings about living during the Vietnam era. So, we decided to take advantage of an opportunity to visit the united nation of Vietnam. Decades would surely have healed our emotions about the turmoil and loss of young lives in the war Americans fought in and lost.

During our visit and tour, the Vietnamese people were warmly welcoming. They are justifiably proud of their nation's post war prosperity. Their nation, with beautiful sandy beaches and a rich history as a French colony is young and optimistic. In fact, some of the best French food we enjoyed was at the La Forchette restaurant in downtown Ho Chi Minh City, formerly Saigon.

But then, we were taken on a tour to the national park near Saigon where the Cu Chi Tunnels are proudly exhibited to show visitors how the North Vietnamese military defeated the mighty Americans. The tunnels were essential to Viet-Cong military operations. They were used by Vietcong soldiers to hide and also served as communication and supply routes, hospitals, food, weapon caches, and living quarters for numerous North Vietnamese fighters. This Vietnamese memorial park is not a renovation to symbolize the war, but is the actual location where the tunnels exist to this day as a source of pride and tribute to the now deceased Ho Chi Minh (1890–1969) and his vision about a military victory.

We were given a paper tri-fold brochure containing a

walking map to help guide us to the many exhibits constructed throughout the historic park. Unbeknown to us, a rifle range is also located adjacent to the exhibits, where those who pay for the experience can fire real M16 rifles, like the ones used by the American military during the war. As we approached the middle of the exhibits while following the tour map, the sounds of bullets suddenly burst forth from the people who were using the M16s in the rifle range. This startling echo from real bullets caused a vivid déjà vu reaction with my husband, whose memory flashed back to Chu Lai. Hearing those chilling rifle sounds while standing in the middle of a Vietnam jungle put him into time traveler mode. My husband's memory was briefly tossed into a vortex where he relived the experience in his past life with the Seabees in Chu Lai. I instantly realized that we had to get beyond those bullets. "Let's get going," I said, when I realized how he was frozen in another time and place. Hearing my voice brought him back. Yet, to this day he recalls the seconds when he was thrust into another dimension. When he heard my voice, he thought, *What is Julie doing in Chu Lai?*

In one of the jungle exhibits, an American army tank was left in place where it had been firebombed by the Vietcong. Most certainly, the young men who were in the tank at the time were killed. It so happened, a group of teenage Australian students were climbing all over the tank and laughing, like kids are prone to do, until I requested for them to please get off. My sincerity alerted them to the reality of the relic left behind. After they left, I took time to meditate about the unknown victims who were inside the tank during the firebombing.

Another time travel experience, albeit with less flashback, occurred during our visit to the moving Vietnam Memorial, when it was in Gardiner, Maine. "The Moving Wall" is the half-size replica of the Washington, DC Vietnam Veterans Memorial and has toured the U.S. for thirty plus years. This moving exhibit includes a screen where vintage

Juliana L'Heureux
Topsham, ME

newsreels about the Vietnam War are shown. This war was the first time when television covered the battles and the dramatic images were watched in black and white on every national evening network newscast. The nightly images and body count reportings caused tremendous backlash to the war in the U.S. and significantly contributed to the campaign to end the conflict.

My husband's Vietnam time travel experiences continue to show up every once in awhile. Most recently, we met David Lyman, author of the book *Seabee 71 in Chu Lai.* Fortuitously, Mr. Lyman happens to live in nearby Camden, Maine. During the Vietnam War, he was a Navy photojournalist. So, my husband was thrust back in time again when we saw, on the very last page of his book, a black and white picture taken with my husband and a group of his Seabee colleagues who were on the runway in Chu Lai, waiting to get on board their C5 military airplane to return home to the base in Davisville, Rhode Island.

Time travel may be the stuff of science fiction, but in our family, the Vietnam War and its aftermath enveloped our lives like being immersed in a history capsule that is loaded with vivid and often difficult memories. I appreciate how my family took the time, while temporarily living in Washington, DC, to visit and meditate at the Vietnam Memorial Wall.

We value the opportunity to reflect about our immersion during our nation's sadly historic era while remembering those who were lost to time.

Stephanie Smith
Camden, ME

The Fog

The other day was clear, now the fog has rolled in,
staying awhile.
Was it yesterday?
Was it today?
What did you say?
I'm in my own way.
Can't find it.
It, whatever it is or was, doesn't matter anyway.
Never mind
the mind.
The fog is in today.

The look, that stare.
lost, are you there,
Somewhere in there?
Gone, trying to find
a safe harbor,
hand holds for your world,
your mind,
in time,
in space.
Blank segments, erased.
The fog may lift, lighten at best.

When we were three,
the time was make-believe.
Reality suspended
until the return to reconnect in time.
Not like now,
a line is fritzed,
the connection doesn't stay, you are off, lost
in a patch of fog.

(continued)

Stephanie Smith
Camden, ME

What did you say?
Never mind, it's ok, no it's not, my refrain.
A tear, and another they're mine, not yours, you lost in
your world, a landmine.

***

Dorothy Hopkins
Waldoboro, ME

The Blackbirds

Early August morning
old moon sinks
pale, lop-sided
mist rises from river
spreads at tree-top level
over old farmland.
Moist air muffles
all sound save my feet
scuffling gravel as I
fetch the morning paper.

Hundreds of blackbirds rise,
The billow of birds wavers
Wings whisper in still air.
Skimming treetops now
Their voices rustle.
They form a line
Head straight north.
May they fly your way
to bring you this gift
they've given me.

Genie Dailey
Jefferson, ME

Meditation on a Maple Tree

Maple tree, you surprise me every spring!
Today I sit on my deck after chores, simply enjoying the
sun,
When suddenly you catch and hold my gaze:
Your crimson buds had appeared without fanfare
(Sometime in the previous twenty-four hours),
And they light the tips of your branches
Like tiny flames that other people never notice.
Against the crystal bluebird sky, those flames stand out,
And I remember why I love you.

Some scoff and call you "swamp maple"—
A peasant among the arboreal royalty known as
"rock maple" and "sugar maple"—
Which are said to be superior
For wood heat and maple syrup.
But I have heated many a cold Maine night with logs
Provided by your brothers and sisters,
And I've made their syrup, too, which won blue ribbons
At the agricultural fair.

Then, in autumn, your leaves linger longer than those
Of the "royal" rock maple in my front yard...
And when they turn color, their brilliant yellow flutters
Like a goldfinch, unique among the duller reds and oranges
Of your forest cousins.
Those who would call you names don't know you
And the gifts you offer the keen observer.
Your crimson buds are just the beginning.

Johanna Engman
Falls Church, VA

A Blade of Grass

It is 2:44 AM on a Saturday morning, and I'm starting up my computer again even though that's exactly what I told myself I shouldn't do. The thing is, I just had an epiphany, and if I don't write it down now it may be gone forever.

I could tell you that I sat on a hill and watched a blade of grass at sunset. And I could say that the grass was emerald green, newly grown, and shiny. I could talk about how its rows of little ridges glinted just so in the light, and that the light itself was golden and thick like honey, like it is in the evening when the sun is setting. I could tell you that that one blade of grass was so beautiful, I looked at it the whole time I was watching, even though there were a million other blades of grass on that very hill. And maybe you would see what I meant, and that it was beautiful.

Or I could tell you that I sat on a hill and watched a blade of grass at sunset. And maybe you would see what I meant, and that it was beautiful.

How is it possible to say the same thing in 13 words that you can say in 107? Perhaps it speaks to the power of the human consciousness, that the human imagination can take 13 words about a blade of grass and turn it into 107 words about emeralds, and ridges, and golden light. Still it goes further, and turns those words into an image in the mind's eye, a feeling in the heart, and a memory of a scent carried on the wind.

And yet, the image is never the same for two people. There's no way to tell what the scent is, because no two bodies carry the same memories within them. The breathtaking complexity of human emotion thwarts any effort of comparing that which lies in two different hearts. I can give you 107 words describing a blade of grass, and still what you see will never be the same as the one I see.

Johanna Engman
Falls Church, VA

Maybe, what you see is just as beautiful. I guess I'll never know.

***

Jean Biegun
Davis, CA

Autumn Games

Flurry of red leaves
two bucks banging new antlers
chill winds referee

Galls on goldenrod
clacking in woodland hailstorms
fall ping pong frenzy

Lilacs in moonlight
saw-whets shuffling on a branch
starting block ready

Besting wide highways
wooly bear caterpillars
long-distance victors

Quick daddy longlegs
scavenging fallen apples
post-game clean-up crew

Peggy Trojan
Brule, WI

Ducks, 1944

We named them
Huey, Dewey and Louie,
after Donald's clan.
They waddled over
the yard all summer,
eating bugs and grass.

In late fall, when they
were grown and fat,
someone stole two.
Pa killed Huey,
which was probably
the original war food plan,
and hung him
upside down
in the cold back porch
to age for a couple of days.

When he appeared
at the table
on Gramma's old platter,
all crispy brown,
minus his head and wide feet,
none of us kids
would eat him.

Jon Olsen
Jefferson, ME

Tree Wisdom

It's October and the trees begin to sleep.
Their slumber lasts till frogs begin to peep.
Their metabolism is so very slow,
Compared to humans, always on the go.
A century for them is not too long,
But few of us get there before the final gong.
I wonder what wisdom they have achieved
Each year before they shed their leaves.
Research now finds they can communicate
Through Nature's own internet, before our starting date.
We have English, Spanish, and Chinese,
So likewise with our friends the trees.
What language have the maples, birch and pines?
And do they speak it softly with some wine
They conjure up from grapes on vine
In pleasure as I do mine?

***

Steve Troyanovich
Florence, NJ

some shadow's hands

Make me this present then: your hand in mine,
and we'll live out our lives in it.

—Michael Donaghy

dreaming in the sleepy language
of yesterdays
you are here
wordless in my heart

Rev. Stephanie J. Batterman
Bath, ME

The Bent-over Woman—
a Story Based on the Gospel of Luke

Luke 13:10–13

10Now he was teaching in one of the synagogues on the
Sabbath. 11And just then there appeared a woman with a
spirit that had crippled her for eighteen years. She was bent
over and was quite unable to stand up straight. 12When
Jesus saw her, he called her over and said, "Woman, you are
set free from your ailment." 13When he laid his hands on her,
immediately she stood up straight and began praising God.

The Bent-over Woman Speaks

My name is Rebekah. That story you just heard is my story. Just look at my back. See how straight it is. Isn't it amazing! A miracle really.

But there is more to my story than what you just heard. I think you will understand better what happened to me if I tell you where I was and what I was thinking on that long-ago Sabbath day.

As usual, I arrived at the synagogue early. I liked to get there before everyone else so I could find a seat near the part that is open to the outside. That way I knew I could get some air. Once the women's portico is full, I found it hard to breathe if I was not near the open air. This was really a problem for them since I was so bent and stooped over.

That day I found a perfect spot and sat down. I probably should have been praying, but instead, I was watching other people arrive. As they neared the synagogue, the men and women split into two groups. The men went into the inner room, but women were not allowed there. So, the women came into the outer portico.

I noticed my younger brother Joshua arrive and follow

Rev. Stephanie J. Batterman
Bath, ME

the men into the holy place. It always surprises me to see him—he is so straight and tall. You should see the way the younger men flock around him and listen to his every word. I am so proud of him. I want to shout, "Look everyone! That is my brother!" But, of course, I don't shout. It wouldn't be seemly. Besides, I didn't want to draw attention to myself. It was humiliating to be so bent over. I could almost hear what people thought about me back then, "Poor woman. I wonder what she did to deserve that infirmity." I wondered about that too. It seemed to me that something inside of me had begun to bend long before my back began to bend. You know what I mean?

Well, that day he noticed me and started to walk toward me. For a brief moment, I was back in our old house when we were young. Joshua and I would sneak up on the roof on hot summer nights. We'd lie there on our backs and look at the stars. We discovered that if we scrunched up our eyes, only the brightest stars would show, and we could make pictures out of the outlines they made in the night sky. We'd talk and laugh and share the secrets of our hearts. We had been such good friends then!

Joshua's voice woke me from my memories. "Becka!" he called. I don't like it when he calls me by that name. I wish he would call me Rebekah. After all, I am a grown woman and older than he is. I want him to show me more respect.

"Little one, how are you?" There he goes again. The names made me angry, but I didn't want to start anything in that place so I answered him, "I'm fine, brother. Now tell me, is it true that that traveling preacher is coming here today? You know the one I mean. I think his name is Jesus."

Joshua stopped walking toward me and looked a bit annoyed. "How do you know about Jesus?" he asked. "You are a woman. You should not be worried about men's concerns. And, by the way," he said, "don't even think about coming near the men's section today. Even I can't keep you out of trouble forever." Then he came close and kissed me

Rev. Stephanie J. Batterman
Bath, ME

on the cheek and patted me on the head, like a person would do to a small child or a pet dog.

Honestly, sometimes he makes me so mad. I don't know why. He's never mean or cruel to me. It's just that we used to be such good friends. How we laughed and played together as children! Back then, I was the one who taught him things. I remembered that time I discovered a new flower down by the stream. It was a tiny pink thing that I had never seen before. I showed Joshua where it was—and the next thing I knew, he was showing it to everyone as if he had discovered it!

I remember the first time he said he was "too big" to play with me. "After all, you are just a girl!" he had said, which broke my heart a little bit.

When Joshua got old enough to study with the rabbi, I had to stay home and help Mother with the housework. At first, he used to run home each day and share with me what he had learned. It had been so exciting to learn about our God. But, one day Father caught us talking about the holy books. He sent me inside to help Mother, but I could hear him shouting at Joshua, "It is not permitted! It is not permitted!" And that had been the end of my education. Joshua never again told me anything he learned from the rabbi.

Mother had seen me crying and tried to make me feel better, "You don't need to know such things. Someone will always take care of you," she said. That had not made me feel better. It just reminded me that I was somehow less than my brother—indeed less than any man.

So, there I was in the women's portico, thinking about all these things. My back was aching again. You know, on that day I couldn't even remember when my back had started to bend.

And, boy, was I tired that day. Not that I had any reason to be so tired. Many people took care of me. Ever since my husband died, I had been living in my father's house. There they didn't expect much from me. They waited on me and

Rev. Stephanie J. Batterman
Bath, ME

pampered me—just as if I was a beloved old pet! I hardly had to think for myself.

Well, I had been sitting in the women's portico thinking about all these things when I was roused by a strange sound. It wasn't really a sound. It was more like a strange silence. I had looked around, but nothing had changed. But, there it was again. I realized that it wasn't a sound or even a strange silence. It was a voice. A man was speaking from the inner room. The voice wasn't loud. It was gentle, but something about it was compelling. I just had to see who was speaking!

I got up from my seat and started moving closer, so I could see who was speaking in such a remarkable way. As I moved, I could feel the heat of the floor stones through my sandals. The sun on my back was warm. It eased the pain in my back a little.

I knew I was getting too close to the inner room. I knew it was forbidden to women, but I could not stop myself. I had to see the man who was speaking. I hoped no one would notice me. Usually, men paid no attention to me at all. I was just a stooped-over harmless thing in their eyes. But I was breaking all the rules by entering the holy part of the synagogue where only men were allowed. I wondered why men thought they were more important than women. I wondered if God really preferred men. Nevertheless, I kept moving toward the forbidden room.

However, in that moment, nothing seemed real but that voice. I could not stop myself. And then, I saw him. I don't know how I knew that he was Jesus. There he was seated and surrounded by other men who were listening to him. Occasionally, one of the men would ask a question. Some seemed angry. But all were listening to him.

I just stood there looking at him. I wasn't really listening. I was just transfixed by him. Suddenly, he looked up. He didn't seem surprised to see me there. He simply motioned for the men to make room for me and I walked right up to him.

Rev. Stephanie J. Batterman
Bath, ME

He stood then and put his hands on my shoulders. "Woman, you are set free from your ailment."

I just stood there. Everything around me was quiet. I had heard his words but did not know what they meant. Then I began to feel a warm heat radiating through my whole self. It seemed to come from a place deep inside me. I looked up and realized that I was looking directly into his eyes. I was standing up straight! I thought I would burst with joy.

Then he reached out and embraced me. I was amazed! He did not condemn me. He did not shout or tell me to leave. He just held me for the longest moment. Then Jesus looked at me with such love and, yes, friendship. No one had looked at me that way, no one had really seen me for a very long time. And I felt whole.

After a long time, I turned from him and faced the other men. They looked angry. Even Joshua had an angry, stormy face as he approached me. Some men were jumping up and starting to speak. They were shouting for me to leave that holy place, that I was just a woman and could not be there.

Out of the corner of my eye, I caught Jesus' eye. In that glance, I knew that we shared a wonderful secret. I looked again at the other men and was amused by them. I felt sorry for them really. You see, I knew something that they did not know. In God's eyes, I was just where I belonged.

***

Sally Belenardo
Branford, CT

Breakfast Still Life

Small, round creamer with
pointed spout, in little bowl:
baby bird in nest.

Helen Stetson
Bluffton, SC

Jubilate Deo Omnis Terra

O be joyful, all the earth

I meandered down to the river
as I am ought to do
and as I slowly ambled
the river rambled too

three white stones
lit a light along the path
under a spreading, shedding
oak tree lay a mushroom cap

a gentle rain was falling
scrubbing pollen from the air
a cleansing for the soul
giving thanks for being there

adjacent to the river grew
twenty-two thin trees
lined along the seawall
leading to a major sea
the river trees reverential
as they bowed their heads in prayer
comforting their fallen limbs
giving thanks for being there

a woman at the seawall
before the crossing of a garter
had been given doctor's orders
to gaze upon salt water
the sea is His for He made it
the earth and every race
dwellers high and lowly
of equal time and space

Helen Stetson
Bluffton, SC

a woman heard a calling
as she walked nearer to the water
her hem reflecting heavenly gold
on God's own living daughter
a buzzing and a humming
from an audience of bees
from four red headed cardinals
applauding from the trees
from fireflies blinking
their tiny fairy lights
a nighthawk's wings dipping
as he took off in flight

the purity of water
on which all life depends
taking care that every mile
of the river never ends
as every single creature
even snails in sandy dirt
every single species
has potential to be hurt

true believers don't have time
to wallow in the muck
to waste their life's potential
protesting in disgust
verily is said to them
pure and tried and true
trust in God with all your heart
just as God has trust in you

Marjorie Arnett
Belfast, ME

Common Ground

Land my family owned
dusted dry my sixteenth summer.
No symphony of rain to turn
the soil a potter's brown.

Like an animal hide
stretched and hung to dry,
ground was parched with no
relief from relentless heat.

I started across the field
that day, hot air like beetle-grit
gnawing my skin. The stink
of small creature-death filled
my nostrils as long strides
took me to my father plowing
in the far west corner.

I saw the snake mounting waves
of scorched ground. We moved
in unison furrow after furrow,
determined soldiers as we cut across
the field, father's lunch pail in hand.

Returning, I saw the snake riding the
field like corrugated cardboard. Cresting
a furrow, disappearing then surface to mount
another blistering ridge of bone-dry land.

Charles Kaska
Heath Springs, SC

No Good

By their deeds you shall know them.
—Matthew 7:16

"One looks like the other so you got to be able to tell them apart." The man shifted in the aluminum folding chair; the boy sat motionless on the wooden step at his feet and stared at the passing cars. The man continued:

> *A hobo is a man down on his luck, looking for work; a bum wants to avoid work and get a handout. Growing up in the Junction, I saw both kinds and plenty of them. They used to jump trains in the Rahway yards and go looking for something to eat. And my mother, your grandma, always had something for them. Our house was known as a 'soft touch' because she treated them well. One of them scratched a mark on the fence, something like this (he drew it in the air but the boy did not look up) so the others would know. But she believed you robbed a man of his dignity if you gave him something and expected nothing in return. So she would ask them to split stove wood. We always needed it because she cooked with it and the stove heated the house in winter. The bos, the good guys, would work till she told them to stop. The bums would say they were too weak and ask to eat first. After they did, they would skedaddle back to the yards and catch the next slow mover.*

"How do you like my chair," inquired the man.

"It's good," replied the boy without enthusiasm.

"I got it for $3.99, a dollar off the original price because I waited for the end-of-season sale. Oh how I wanted that chair! But I wouldn't buy it because I knew it would be marked down when summer was almost over and people

Charles Kaska
Heath Springs, SC

were thinking about Fall. It's all about knowing how to handle your money—not throwing it away. That's what the bo and the bum have in common: they don't know how to handle their money. If they did they wouldn't be bos and bums," he added with a smile.

A passer-by inquired, "On vacation, Basil?"

"Yeah," laughed the man, "on vacation."

The passer-by nodded, "Enjoy" and continued on his way.

"Another way you can tell the bum from the bo is if they put the bite on you, offer to buy them food. The bo will take it and be grateful. The bum will refuse and insist on the money. He doesn't want food; he just wants to buy a drink. He's just..." the man paused searching for the right word, "no good."

"I got to go," said the boy, "I got a job weeding for 75 cents an hour."

"Sure, go ahead kid. That's the spirit. Go get 'em." He watched the boy saunter down the street till he turned the corner.

Basil felt satisfied. His son was industrious; anyone could see that. He had given the boy another important lesson in how to judge people and it was plain he understood. His wife had a part-time job as a clerk-typist with an insurance company. His unemployment had another six weeks to go. He had had an egg fried in bacon grease for lunch. He cooked it himself but left the pan in the sink for his mother-in-law: "Her house. Her pan. Her cleanup." He patted the arm of the folding chair, reached under it and retrieved *The Daily Mirror.* He folded it back to expose just the page listing the upcoming races and began to study the odds. For an instant he was annoyed that the page was distorted by his paunch but assured himself, "All men get that." A breeze caressed his shoulders exposed by his sleeveless undershirt. "It's gonna be cool tonight," thought Basil, "good sleeping weather."

Lou Bolster
Fairfield, IA

By Design

I sat on a rock at the side of the path.
It was one of those times.
Those times when I am
Overcome by the beauty around me.
Overcome by emotions inside.

Emotions of love, for everyone and everything.
Emotions of fear and grief that I will lose it all.
Emotions of gratitude that I can't lose it all.

All at once. Stirred up inside.
I wept. I felt I would break.

Thinking I was alone, I said aloud;
"How can I go on? Feeling all of this?"

The one sitting next to me gently said;
"Oh, you'll figure it out.
You see, you were designed for this. To feel this.
All of this. All at once even.
Yes, you were built for this."

The tip of a wing flicked my leg.
A gentle wind caressed my face.
And I knew.
And I didn't feel quite so brittle.

Emily Blair Stribling
Brooklin, ME

Sold

Swan's Island

This is the island
where we watched the whales,
my grandmother holding my hand
hooted with joy as
a great blue hulk
launched itself into the air
and splashed wildly down.

This is the island
where wild roses roamed
the old stone wall we climbed
to follow the path to the sea
to swim in the heart-stopping
Maine water, the stony beach
warm under our feet.

This is the island
where every August
the family gathered on the porch
to celebrate my mother's birthday
gorging on lobsters, fresh corn
and chocolate cake. Always
afterwards our parents napped.

This is the island
where I had thought my children
would bring their children
to watch the whales.
But they married and scattered,
moved to cities and
watch movies instead.

Emily Blair Stribling
Brooklin, ME

This is the island
where I came to accept
a house needs voices and
laughter, poems and stories,
waking and sleeping,
not absence and stillness,
not light dying in the corner.

This is the island
where today I stare at
black and white photos
of the house and an old barn
taken before I was born.
Tomorrow I will send them
to the new owner.

***

Cordula Mathias
Trevett, ME

Helpless...

Now you must learn to
Help less
Now you must learn to
Let go
You must learn to
Let uncertainty
Rule the hours
Of the remaining days

Bunny L. Richards
Trescott Twp., ME

Dying of the Light

In the weary month,
winter fast approaches.
Red speckled leaves
like dried blood lie
among wind-plastered
pine needles pushed
into cracked asphalt.

Dead lined bark peels
from moose maple, birch,
to reveal brown rot,
worm dung,
cavities where
nuthatch and downy
hunt hidden feed.
Living sky bleeds steadily.

Mourning doves prowl
with tick covered squirrels
on spattered ground,
while white rabbits
stark against dark fields
attract the gaze of hawks.

Olive C. Hart
Newcastle, ME

Lakeshore Camp

For Us Three Little Kids, as Judy, Lois and I called ourselves, the mornings at camp followed a routine, not governed by time. Clocks at the lake had little significance, so it became solely a sequence of events.

First was the trip to the Little House, still in p.j.'s. Nobody but family for miles, so no need for a robe. Breakfast was next, then dishes and making beds. Dressing was simple: not clothes, only bathing suits for spending the rest of the morning in and around the lake. The part we dreaded was the edict in those days that after eating you had to wait an hour before going in the water. Going sooner could cause some calamity for sure—cramps? sinking? drowning?

Now and then some kid, usually a boy, would brag that he had done it. We were never sure whether it was the truth or was a big lie, but nobody I knew offered to test it.

Younger folks wouldn't know that our bathing suits were made of wool. I have no idea why, but in theory it sounds all right, doesn't it? The proof, however, was in the wearing. After just a few hours in the wet suits our inner thighs would be chafed red and sore. Sometimes toward the end of the morning, we shed the suits and played in the water naked.

Our Victorian mother would have objected, but she had seen and treated the sore places. We were in the water more than out, and it was nearly lunch time, so she allowed it.

Then came Daddy's vacation. While the rest of the family was at camp, he had been with us only for the weekend and Wednesday night. He made the early morning trips to Bangor on Monday and Thursday to be back in his office on the job as an electrical engineer at Bangor Hydro-Electric where he worked until his retirement. But he was happiest at camp. He loved the outdoors, nature in all seasons and aspects. He taught us the names of the trees, the kinds of wild flowers, rocks, and mosses—lots of things I still remember.

During his vacation he had plans for what he wanted to do himself or with the family, even with Us Three Little Kids. One day he had put on his bathing suit and was standing up to his waist in water when he called to me to come over. "It's time you learned to swim."

Right away I was whining, "Do I have to? We were playing...."

"It won't take long," he assured me. "Come and try it; it'll be fun."

Well, it sounded more like a chore to me, but when Daddy told me to do it there wasn't any choice.

First Daddy wanted me to float. Float? Everybody knows people don't float. That's why they swim!

But I had to try. So I lay back in the water for just seconds, then scrambled to my feet to report, "My feet keep sinking, and there's water in my ears."

Daddy was reassuring right away, "It's all right if the feet sink a little. Are the ears all right now?" I nodded, and he said, "Let's try again. You can feel my hand under your back, can't you?"

I did a little better that time, and won his approval.

"That's fine. Now turn the other side up."

"Daddy, I don't...."

"It's all right. I'm here. You are going to do the Dog Paddle."

"I am?" I giggled at that; it sounded so silly. Swim like a dog!

Daddy showed me how to close my fingers together to pull the water, and then he held the straps of my bathing suit in the back while I leaned forward into the water.

"Now start paddling your hands and kicking your feet."

"I'll try, but don't let go," I begged.

"I've got you," he said. "Go ahead and paddle."

I thrashed hard for a while, keeping both hands and feet going. When I put my feet on the bottom and turned to ask if I was doing it right, Daddy wasn't near.

"Daddy, you said you would hang on to me."

"Well, I couldn't. See where you are? You swam right away from me," he said with a big smile.

"But you promised.......wait. You mean I was really swimming?"

"All the way, by yourself."

I was amazed. I had concentrated on keeping both hands and feet working, but it wasn't really hard. And I was swimming! I went back over to Daddy to have him start me off again. This time I headed for Judy and Lois.

"Hey, look at me! I'm really swimming!" My sisters thought I splashed a lot, but their praise was generous and sincere. We celebrated together that day, and it was not long before their turns came. (I think Daddy conned them about the suit straps the same way he did me. We all fell for it. It worked over and over.)

Anyway, we all became swimmers, nothing of championship style, but competent to ease the minds of both our parents, leaving us all free to come and go around the water wherever we pleased.

Some years later, Judy did pull off an impressive feat, swimming from our dock all the way across the lake to the opposite shore with Richard alongside to supervise. I really admired her for that and thought I would like to try it some day, too. Although that never did come to pass, I have never lost the admiration for Judy's feat, and her record in our family still stands un-challenged.

So our days at camp were tranquil. There were many ways in which we could have been injured: in the deep water, on the slippery rocks, lost in the woods, or climbing the pine tree. We found or invented new adventures, but we ended each season tanned and healthy, stronger than ending the last one.

We were reluctant to close camp in September, knowing of the long months before another spring. Still, in the mean-

Olive C. Hart
Newcastle, ME

time we anticipated making new friends, going to a different school perhaps, and there would be snow, skating, winter fun, and best of all, Christmas.

Our winter life began again.

***

Marjorie Arnett
Belfast, ME

Maine Memory

I remember an uncle
sitting on our swing
he was three axe handles
across the behind,
the swing only one.

It looked unpleasant
rope cutting into his skin
like that. He didn't seem
to notice, kept on talking,
pushing his feet into the dirt.

I remember on a hot day
jumping in the swimming hole,
spring fed and ice cold
it made your legs go numb.

Mom always said, as I came
shivering into the house,
What possible pleasure
could that bring you,
your skin all goose bumps.

Margaret Roncone
Vashon, WA

At the California Coast

During summer months
the Indian Roller feeds
late into the evening
making use of artificial light to feed on
the insects they attract.

The sea rolls without remorse
high tide; small sailboats
are strewn on the beach
like driftwood
masts, compasses pointing northwest
cabins rocked and wrecked with
navigational charts,
empty soup cans, bits
of a voyager's last dream

we watch from the safety
of a small car
windshield wipers spreading sea foam like
icing on a wedding cake
beauty is found in the terror of the sea

"We are guests here" my sister-in-law tells
me

ten years of ocean swimming living in her
voice
we drive the highway as it floods from a
nearby stream
I taste salt water in falling rain.

Abby Ingraham
Bristol, ME

The Pearl

Life for some
is all welcome mats
and the world is My Oyster

While others find
only barbed wire
and No Vacancy signs

While I stand,
deeply scratched
but ecstatic,
With The Pearl in my hand

***

Mary Ann Bedwell
Grants, NM

Ephemera

The shadow a blown-glass paperweight throws
        as it sits on the shelf—
        Footprints in the snow,
        Smoke from a campfires glow,
        A whiff of perfume.
Some things, when they occur,
        You know they will soon be gone.

Enjoy these things while they are here,
        Hold fast to that which you hold dear;
You must learn that life goes on,
        A flock of birds flying overhead

Carole Cochran
Boothbay Harbor, ME

The Age of Innocence

When my boyfriend said, "You'll never get near him," it raised my hackles and heightened my determination. *HE* was coming to Baltimore, on a campaign stop at the Emerson Hotel. Carefully, I chose my outfit for the event: white gloves, pearl earrings, low heels, a green floral print dress with its wide self-belt. Driving my blue Volkswagen convertible, I arrived downtown with my high hopes and a good parking space.

At the age of 18, I was unable to vote, but this candidate sparked an interest in politics that continues to this day. His youth! His intelligence! His glamour! His wife! His family! His humor! His tan! He inspired in me a lifelong yearning for learning. After years of boring Ike and Mamie, this man brought youth and exuberance to the national arena. And boy, did I have youth and exuberance to spare. He inspired me with his words, with his composure, with his humor, with his "gray matter," which was a favorite phrase of my English teacher. "Girls, read and read and read. Use up that gray matter before it is gone."

During this exciting time, I began reading newspapers. I *craved* information about the election, about the candidate. This led to following national and local events. This led to comparing the candidates, reading both sides of an issue, and forming opinions based on facts. Walter Cronkite and CBS News was another source.

On the night of the campaign stop, *he* arrived looking trim, handsome, and tan. I could see him clearly from my second row seat. Just a pit stop for him, but a magical moment for me. At the end of the speech, the audience rose to their feet, and some stood on their chairs. My "youth and exuberance" helped me to do the same thing. It also helped me to reach out to his outstretched hand, with glove off.

Carole Cochran
Boothbay Harbor, ME

My trip home was uneventful, but my boyfriend was amazed with my pluckiness. I began passing out fliers, posting campaign posters, knocking on doors, and urging residents to vote. I followed the debates on TV, the convention speeches, and of course the election. My roommate and I stayed up all night to get the results. We watched the young senator and his pregnant wife being interviewed the following morning at their Georgetown home. We watched the inauguration, the evening dances, the glitz and the glamour.

This was a time of deep emotions, trust, hope, and a celebration of intelligence and creativity. It was a time when voters changed their opinions about candidates by listening and by reading and by conversing with others who were not like-minded. My dad was from the south, and was a Democrat. *But*, he was anti-Catholic. After the election, he confessed that he had voted for the Catholic candidate. Why? He, too, listened and read and asked questions. My enthusiasm might have encouraged him, too.

In these current troubled days of politics, of the viral spiral of radio and television and internet, there is little rational discourse. The age of innocence is gone. The man who inspired me is gone. After his early death, and the international sadness, it was written that, "We'll never laugh again." The rejoinder was, "No, we'll never be young again."

***

Mary Ann Bedwell
Grants, NM

Owl

Among bright Spring green
The owl surveils the Bantam
Barred by rabbit wire.

Celine Rose Mariotti
Shelton, CT

How Will the World End?

I wonder lately,
All the time,
Because nothing rhymes,
How will the world end?
What will God send?
This Pandemic has changed
Our world; our reality,
A certain complexity,
The war in the Ukraine
Continues on,
Russia, China and North Korea
Threatening nuclear war on
The dark horizon,
We have to pray for some
Kind of sanity,
Shootings every day,
People in a state of anxiety,
Panic attacks have become
A part of life,
Getting by financially
Causes people strife,
So how will the world
End one day?
None of us knows
We just have to
PRAY!

Bill Herring
Minnetonka, MN

Out Here at Corhaven Graveyard

Out here near Holmans Creek
the bones of Old Jack remain at rest
beyond the delta waves of sleep
out here beneath these sacred trees
with their barbed-wire scars out here
among the white violets, the snails that slime
across the crumbling fieldstones
and broken dream headstones.

Out here, Old Jack, first name only
following the gray-haired adjective.
No middle initial, no last name,
no date of birth or death certificate.
No indication of who he was other than *slave.*

Out here there are others. Reuben. Tom.
Toby. Sue. And Nan and her child.
Two deaths that beg for a backstory.
Did they die together? And how? You can't ask
the ghosts of the gravediggers.
Their voices are silent now, like the clouds
over those treetops, like the moon
lighting their leaves, like the silicon dust
that fills the Sea of Tranquility.

Out here you'll find Winney. Jenny. Ann
and Old Nan. You'll find biblical names
like James and John. Samuel of the Old Testament
and Mary of the New. But these were neither
disciples, nor prophets, nor mothers of God.
They were ordinary folk like you,
like me, but with just one name. Like Noah.
Abraham. Like Ruth. Like Jesus.

Bill Herring
Minnetonka, MN

Out here you'll find Doll. George. Sall
and others, *always others.* Our grandmothers,
our grandfathers sleeping deep
beneath these sacred trees, among
these white violets, these snails that slime
across the crumbling fieldstones
and broken dream headstones
on what was once a plantation on a backroad

out here in the Shenandoah Valley.

***

Rebecca Brooks
Topsham, ME

Knowing

I once imagined
that the Old Man
still watched over a giant
sleeping in the Pemigewasset.
The forest vibrated
at a rapid pitch—
different somehow.
And I could feel them humming.
Those who I talk to
in my reverie.
Too soon have they gone
like the Old Man.
But I am here.
A giant
dreaming
to never wake up.

Thomas Peter Bennett
Silver Spring, MD

Squirrel Routine

A squirrel emerged
        from its winter lodge,
three stories up,
        in a hollow dead branch,
of a wild cherry tree,
        and surveyed.

A man and woman sat at a table,
        by a window,
in a red brick building
        with an attached balcony.

The squirrel leaped
        to the window ledge,
and startled the couple,
        before scampering
along the brick siding
        toward the balcony.

A jump to the balcony railing,
        and up a pole
to a bird feeder and seeds.
        The balcony door slammed,
and the man stood,
        clapping his hands,
as the squirrel jumped
        from the feeder to the railing.

An agile jump to the brick siding. . .
        steps and jumps repeated,
in reverse order. . .
        back to the tree's hollow dead branch,
with squirrel jowls filled with seeds.

Judy Driscoll Winchenbaugh
Rockland, ME

Sea Treasures

The letter from Great Aunt Anna crinkles in my pocket. My fingers are twitching, impatient to open the envelope that has traveled across the country to reach our Nebraska farm.

The sun is so hot this morning, the thermometer on our barn reads ninety-five degrees. Will this drought ever end? The ground under my feet feels as parched as my throat. Chores seem endless, I gather eggs, milk the cows, let them out to the pasture that's no longer lush and green. Then I have to muck the barn, churn the butter and try to mend my good church dress again.

Pastor Brown says keeping busy will stop me from missing my Charlie, but I say he is wrong. Oh, I am so proud of him, fighting for our country, fighting to keep it whole, not split us into two countries.

Finally, morning chores are done. Time to sit and read Great Aunt Anna's letter. A small glass of water from the well, a rocking chair on the porch and a letter to read. Yes, Pastor Brown I am grateful and count my blessings. And now I have this letter that traveled from Maine to Nebraska. I wonder, how many trains and stagecoaches were needed to transport this letter to me. Finally, I can open it.

June 30, 1865

My Dear Suzanna,

I hope this letter finds you well. I'm afraid I do have some sad news to convey. Your great-grandmother passed away peacefully in her sleep last week. I will be writing separately to your mother, my sister, the sad news. Grandmother will be missed as we mourn her passing.

You were just a little girl when your parents left

Judy Driscoll Winchenbaugh
Rockland, ME

Maine for Nebraska. But Grandmother never forgot you; she always remembered your bright red curls and feisty independence. I can still hear her chuckling: 'Suzanna gets her hair and temper from my Frank, God rest his soul. I pity anyone who crosses her path when that little girl is grown!'

I am sure your independence has helped you run the farm since Charles left for the war. I understand your parents' property is not far from yours. Please know your husband is in our prayers and we hope you are soon blessed with his return.

Grandmother left you one of her greatest treasures which I am sending to you separately. It is not valued in money but in sentiment. She asked that her collection of sea treasures from our beach be given to you, so that you don't forget your Maine roots and maybe, someday, you and Charlie will come home to us.

She always said there is a story behind each shell, sea glass, or broken piece of pottery, which I will try to remember as I describe what is in the small wooden chest she kept on her dresser.

First is an ordinary snail shell, about a half inch in length, mostly shades of gray and white. There is a small opening underneath and the top twirls to a point. I remember her telling me an empty house is the same as an empty snail shell, just waiting for its occupants to make it a home again.

Next you will see a piece of sea glass, broken and worn down by the waves and tides of the ocean. This one is blue, a rare find, about three inches long. Hold it up to the light and you'll see the letters 'OO' and 'MORE MD,' what is left of the writing on the bottle. It reminds me of Grandfather's elixir bottles he always hid in the shed!

There is also a piece of brown crockery, such as a piece of mother's old beanpot. When I was young and

Judy Driscoll Winchenbaugh
Rockland, ME

woke up to the smell of beans baking in the cookstove I knew it was Saturday! We still follow the New England tradition of beans, brown bread, biscuits and cabbage salad on Saturday nights.

You'll see two more pieces of crockery. One is rounded with blue and green stripes; I imagine a woman somewhere used it to mix her bread dough. The other piece has a blue and white pattern; I think it is a Blue Willow piece. Do you know the story of the young couple escaping from the girl's tyrant father? It's a story made famous on Blue Willow china.

Next is a small limpet shell—it looks like a chinaman's hat. When the limpet is living inside the shell it sticks to a rock with a very strong suction. And it is very sharp under bare feet, as I have discovered!

Then there is a lady slipper shell. My favorite. A very ordinary shell until you turn it over. Half the inside has a shell across it, like a shelf, which leaves a small opening. My Great Grandmother Levensaler used to tell us Mother Nature made them so fairies could wear the shells as slippers, to dance in on the beach under the stars.

Lastly, you will find what looks like a stopper to a glass perfume bottle. Do you know those beds with carved pineapples on the bedposts? The stopper looks just that, and the glass is worn down to a milky white color. The perfume bottle probably adorned a lady's dressing table to be used for special occasions.

That is enough rambling, I will arrange to have this box shipped to you. I hope it brings you a little closer to all of us back in Maine and reminds you of the love Great Grandmother had for you.

All my love,

Great Aunt Anna

Judy Driscoll Winchenbaugh
Rockland, ME

I put the letter back in my apron pocket, dreaming of standing on the rocky shore, the sea stretching as far as I can see, feeling the breeze and tasting that tangy salt air. Is it a memory or my imagination drawn from Great Aunt Anna's descriptions?

I stand up, go inside to start my dinner. In the distance I hear a horse galloping, dust rising behind it. If it was only Charlie on that horse, coming home to me. Ahh, my imagination is working overtime again. I go inside, shutting the door behind me.

***

Marjorie Arnett
Belfast, ME

Ruminate

On the front of a dog-eared page,
two mirrors face each other. It was
our 19th day reading Alice Luttermen's
book written in self-help code. A manual
for followers of human delusions,
mediations on cause, addictions and
how to make coffee with essential
ingredients. Issue 512–August. Page 21.
Measuring time. We buy a kitchen timer,
find a store that sells meditation supplies
and a French press and begin to sink into
deep digression. *Raw Eggs* my mantra,
Annoying Kindness, his. Watch by
my side, minds like shredding bolts,
we sit together searching for stillness.
I expected it to happen as the greyhound
drank vodka on the 23rd day.

Robert B. Moreland
Pleasant Prairie, WI

In Like a Lion

Sound overwhelms him long before he sees
the east wind gusts driving huge lake breakers.
He finds his way with care down to the beach,
half-moon enshrouded by threatening clouds.

In the dark, he feels spray swept from the crests.
As his eyes adjust to the night, he sees
scores of whitecaps form and dissolve westward.
Crashing surf smacks beach barricades, misting.

The noise deafening as squadrons of swells
rise and grow to disappear, meet the shore.
Northward, Kenosha Harbor blurs in spray,
stormy sea, Wind Point Light flashes then gone.

High water mark washed away as waves surge;
sand wet, dries to ruddy dullness again.
As the onslaught continues, parka soaked,
he recalls March Atlantic storms back east.

Great lake stretches beyond his horizon,
his mortality clear facing this gale.
How do the captains navigate these storms?
In awe of the majesty, he hikes home.

Moreland, R.B. (2021) "In Like a Lion" in *Ariel Anthology 2021*
Edited by Jan Chronister and Lucy Tyrell, page 16.

Carol Leavitt Altieri
Lakewood Ranch, FL

Coming Back to Madison from West Coast of Florida

Stranded between two homes, shedding
my outgrown shell,
I feel the siren call back to Madison.
Later, I'm unmoored by anxiety
as my marine friend with astonishing intensity,
applauds the enhancements of Florida.
So I settle into my hometown state
where I have lost many cherished ones.
Triggers pull me back into times of trauma.

Like a sea creature I hunker down to the Shoreline life,
feeling the tropics again as 90 degree humidity
soaks into my skin.
And saddened at the ever-shifting swirling dance
of life and death as my friends have passed.
Poaching in L.I. Sound, a gray sparrow hawk
rises over the marsh, shoots a sharp look at me
to set the world right.
The sun spreads multi-colored jewels across
the Hammonassett River.

I visit the mud flats where I used to go birding
hear the endangered seaside sparrow;
see the piping plovers' protected nests
by Friends of Hammonasset.

Recapturing joy, I return to the Friday and Saturday
night tribes that welcome me to the dance bands
at Scotland Plains, Madison Beach and Water's Edge
and hip-hop away the hours.

Carol Leavitt Altieri
Lakewood Ranch, FL

A narcissist promises me the moon and the stars.
Wolves invade my pen. I correct blind spots
and try to prevent the wolf from the injured sheep.
(I want to know how a wolf thinks
and to know when I see one.)

I hike out to Willard's Island and smell
the fragrance of sweet pepperbush
rising over the soil, transporting me to other
summers. Cerulean, golden and orange butterflies'
nectar among the Indian paint brushes.
A jewelwing damselfly with green wings delights
me as I watch it.

The old house next door is still abandoned
looking haunted and overgrown with poison ivy.
Mice and chipmunks raise families underground
gorging on seeds from the bird feeder.
Clumps of birch trees with sheets of bark peeling,
hold mocking birds mimicking alarms.
Crickets' incessant sounds join the Post Rd. cacophony.

I have returned home with fresh eyes,
to my deepest reconnections to Earth

Erine Leigh
Portsmouth, NH

Bitten, Blues

Circle of wild lupines,
Attended by bees.
Royal, purple-blue, cream-white, pink,
Paranormally exquisite.

Well-rested but ravaged,
Bitten by the written word,
Unsteady, bidden, slowed,
Found in the place lupines stir.

Under bluebird skies on coves and inlets
Of whale-blue ocean, pith of creation,
Blues ever forage, cerulean supplication.

Like the crow and the angel,
Like the lonely storm,
What survives on island
Is stem-cell sworn.

Janice Babcock
Wauwatosa, WI

My First Car

In 1963, I was beginning my one year clinical internship and needed to be at the hospital at 7:00 a.m. I needed a car; otherwise, I would have had to take a bus which meant transferring twice. I really needed a car.

I went with my parents to a nearby used car lot and immediately fell in love with a vivid turquoise convertible. This car had class and pizzazz, suitable for a soon to be college senior. The car was a Metropolitan, an American Motors product made in England. I paid $400.00 for the car with some help from my parents.

When my family moved to Milwaukee, they removed a rickety garage on their property. There was space for a two car garage but built one that was smaller. Unfortunately, they did not foresee their daughter in need of a car in a few years. Our house did not have a driveway; behind the house there was an alley. To accommodate parking for the second car, my father laid stone blocks on the grass in the back yard. Winter was fast approaching. I purchased a canvas tarp to cover my convertible car roof to keep it free of snow and ice at night and removed the tarp every morning. Ugh!

Our family car had an automatic transmission but mine had a tricky stick shift which would get stuck somewhere between gears. When that happened, I would pull over to the side of the road and lift the car's hood. I always carried a hammer on the seat next to me which I would use to align the gears, allowing me to drive again.

At the hospital where I worked, I would drive my car to a popular custard stand on the south side of Milwaukee with my colleagues. On the northwest side of Milwaukee, the same thing happened with my friends. I had a car and drove them to a different custard stand.

Memories of my first car resurfaced about thirty years

Janice Babcock
Wauwatosa, WI

ago at my college reunion. Everyone remembered that I was a woman who owned her own car. My friends ogled my turquoise car and clamored for a ride.

After my internship ended, I traded in my cute convertible and bought a used American Motors Rambler with automatic transmission. However, I will always remember my first sporty turquoise convertible.

***

Mary Ann Bedwell
Grants, NM

The Taste of Music

The seats in the concert hall
remind me of brown papers in a box,
each one the home to a different delight.
I take my place and wait impatiently
for the luscious treat to begin.
First the oboe, holding out a long note
for the tuning, "Anitra's Dance"
the spiral of a candy cane against the snow.
Black jelly beans drip from the bell
of the instrument warming up
for Mozart's clarinet concerto.
The high, taut voice of the concert master's instrument
brings a bag of lemon drops into harmony,
joining the violas, smooth and melting
as a Hershey Bar on a hot summer day.
The French horns pour their caramel
over a bowl of butter pecan ice cream
as the bassoon, hidden somewhere in the middle,
raises the horehound stick of "Rite of Spring."

Sylvia Little-Sweat
Wingate, NC

Ruins

Before a dallying Tudor king broke
with Rome to divorce his Catholic
queen to marry pregnant Anne Boleyn,
Cistercian monks—habited in undyed
wool—had for centuries kept Tintern
Abbey's rooms as safe as wombs.
At Henry's command, Cromwell pulled
churches and abbeys down, pilfered
coffers, stabled horses in sanctuaries.

Four centuries hence, the Abbey's gray
walls and turrets of stone stand lichen-
etched, roofless in a vale in Wales.
Arches breach a vaulted sky, form ledges
where white doves shelter from wind
and rain. Swallows swoop at will to nave
and transept, their flitting wings silent
now as Mass and Matins past—no altar
but the dark for prayers at Evensong.

***

Michelangelo

To gaze on David's face
the moment before
his stone will slay
Goliath or on Mary's
as she holds her son
is to chisel marble death—
just before and after.

Tamara Kittredge
Vashon, WA

Tree Dreams

There are dreams attached like bark to the skin of you.
Dreams set aside by circumstance,
they wait in the shade of time
holding fast with the feet of trees
plunged deep into the soil of the soul.
Dreams forming a basket of expectant branches
reaching upwards into a squandered sky.
Fragile dream fingers poised for a time not yet come
to catch the falling moment.
In my dreams I catch the leaf of you
finally blown free by a sympathetic breeze.
I look skyward to see your spiraling gracefulness
of red and gold making way into my astonished hands
I cup the treasure of you close to my breath
and marvel at your colors, and scent while tracing
the outline of you with a gentle loving fingertip.

***

Ukraine's Collective Sorrow

Our birth cries were silenced,
aborted by the piling of the victor's stones
over the womb of humanity.
Ukraine destroyed while the expectant world labored,
Mid scream, ears filled with the noise of too much
and of not enough.
What was Ukraine, now a mosaic moonscape
of greys, browns, and black rubble.
Numbed by the impossibility of the senseless dead
our collective freedom buried under the
victor's well-placed stones.

Judith L. Braun
Alfred, ME

Octopus

An Octopus has tentacles and so does war! This soft eight-limbed undulating creature with two eyes and one mouth is capable of multiple configurations. It can transport itself in one long body or engage the multiple limbs in several directions. It can squeeze through small gaps, is very intelligent and diverse in behavior. They can live deep in the ocean or in the shallow water of high and low tide. They sting emitting a venomous toxic liquid. Two of the eight tentacles are used for walking, the other six for foraging food. The arms can extend, contract, bend, or twist, each has circular, adhesive suckers. The suckers allow the octopus to anchor itself or to manipulate objects. Two large eyes are at the top of the head. The brain is similar to a human brain, breathes oxygen, ingests food and expels. Octopuses are predators searching for food in small crevices. Being highly intelligent and to protect themselves from larger predators, they can camouflage themselves in an inky blot.

I use this symbol for war, specifically the Vietnam War. While many young men and women were choosing to enter a "tentacle" of the Armed Services, others were being preyed upon by another tentacle of mandatory conscription. Each was under the guise of "feeding" the good of the main body, the USA. Tentacles representing Air Force, Army, Marines, Coast Guard, and Navy, each had a specific mission of feeding the head of the octopus.

The octopus of war, clearly capable of squeezing into small places, interrupted my life more than once. It first appeared in my life and thousands of others' across the United States who were graduating from high school in 1965. It changed the course of many coming-of-age baby boomers. The Draft brought the war to the American home front. During the Vietnam War era, between 1964 and 1973, the

Judith L. Braun
Alfred, ME

U.S. military drafted 2.2 million American men out of an eligible pool of 27 million. Although only 25 percent of the military force in the combat zones were draftees, the system of conscription caused many young American men to volunteer for the armed forces in order to have more of a choice of which division in the military they would serve. As if that would stop the predator octopus. At the time, these statistics never registered in my life. History says draftees mostly came from working class towns. I grew up in Wadsworth, Ohio, never thought of it as working class but I guess it was. All men 18 years and older had to register with the Selective Service. They were eligible to be drafted for a service requirement of 21 months. This was followed by a commitment for either 12 consecutive months of active service or 36 consecutive months of service in the reserves, with a statutory term of military service set at a minimum of five years total. Conscripts could volunteer for military service in the regular United States Army for a term of four years or the Organized Reserves for a term of six years.

A magnetic attraction had always existed between my guy, Gary, and me. He was drafted and inducted in 1967. Basic training and three months of Officer Candidate School qualified him to lead troops. He was an artillery man, safe behind the infantry ground troops, I was told. In the spring of 1968, he received his orders for Vietnam. He was on leave for a month before deploying. We saw each other frequently and wrote letters once he was gone. Worry, fear, anticipation moved into my life calmed only when a letter arrived in the mail. Always, I opened with the fear that he might be dead while I was reading his last letter. Early summer the letters stopped. My worry and concern kicked into high gear. What happened? A short conversation with his mother revealed that he had been granted permission to come home from the war to marry the girl he got pregnant while stationed in Maryland. My hopes and dreams were swallowed in the bowels of the octopus of war. Now, my pride of military service

Judith L. Braun
Alfred, ME

turned to anger. This war, this octopus, that saturated our living room TV and radio news had now twisted into my personal life.

I set about creating my own life dodging the tentacles. Three years later, 1970, we both attended our first high school class reunion. He and I met privately. Catchup conversation revealed two unhappy quarreling parents of a toddler. A month or so later the letters began to flow furiously between us. He and his wife had divorced. We married six months later. I willingly, and knowingly, accepted military life with the tentacles of war still close.

Sure as an octopus preys for food, Vietnam raised its ugly head again as he received orders to return for another year of duty. I would return to Ohio to wait and worry. The octopus's life was beginning to wane (1972) and his orders were changed to Germany. Two years of marriage to a war-torn man saw many battles between us. My commitment to honor marriage and the allure of a European adventure sent me across the Atlantic to spend three years and three months in Germany.

Our son was born on the night that the Vietnam War ended. April 30–May 1, 1975. At long last, I thought the war would stop interfering with my/our life. Riding home from the hospital with son in my arms, father at the wheel. The world looked different; a paradigm shift was taking place within my soul. No war, a son to raise, surely our magnetic marriage would find a solid connection as parents. I thought the octopus had lived its life.

However, a tentacle of an off-spring lived in my house in the form of PTSD! My husband's anger grew many tentacles in the span of twenty-five years with treatment denied or unavailable; we divorced. The final sleuthing tentacle of agent orange caused lymphoma and took his life.

A tentacle of this war reached me again when a friend's story revealed that her husband died on the battlefield, leaving a young woman to raise three sons.

Judith L. Braun
Alfred, ME

The many nurses that served under some tentacle buried the brutal visions of war because no one wanted to admit they had participated in this unpopular war.

The circular suckers of the tentacles stuck to many returning from the war zone and were denied any recognition and even spit on if they entered the USA in uniform. The octopus' suckers of war appeared in lives as PTSD nightmares. It was 10–15 years before the government admitted it by establishing programs to heal the inward wounds of war.

I was reminded, at a memorial service in Washington, DC in October 2021, just how far the off-spring of the original octopus tentacles stretched over many lives and stories. Five hundred family members read the name of a soldier who, as a result of their service, died later. He was honored, finally, with a WELCOME HOME!

***

Steve Troyanovich
Florence, NJ

Thanksgiving Poem for John Trudell

within the shelter of your words
dreams entered
the vocabulary of immaculate dawn
fragments of light
clutching absence and memory
between the infinite music
of an eagle's wing

Peggy Trojan
Brule, WI

Spare Change

We did not get an allowance
In the forties,
when a bottle of pop or a candy bar
cost a nickel,
We did chores around the house
like a penny for a swatted fly.
(A job which ended when Pa
discovered that we were killing
flies on the outside of the screen door.)
The ideal place for change was between
the brown Mohair couch cushions after Pa's
daily noon nap on a lunch break,
as manager of the general store.
Looking back now, I suspect he
was intentionally leaving some extra
change, knowing how delighted we
would be upon discovery.

***

Lou Bolster
Fairfield, IA

Oh Grief

Oh grief
Tread lightly on me
Allow me the space to remember
Not that I may hang onto the past
But that I adjust for the future
Even embrace the future
Of my new reality

Sylvia Little-Sweat
Wingate, NC

Woman by the Sea*

Marie Celeste gazes upon
a distant line where sky
meets sea endlessly.

Once she was free
to feel winds
lash her heart
and waves break white
upon her breasts.
On brightest days at sea
she rode the prow
to quicken foam
and furrow waves
for the wheeling gulls,
and as winds clanged
the rigging of the sails
on blackest ocean swells,
from the mast
she scanned the deep
for stormy blasts.

Moored now
to an Isla Negra beam,
chained at last to shore,
she longs for bracing winds
and surging waves
a moaning sea
once more.
Still, in the wake of winter
though sheltered from the sea
tears form
in her crystal eyes,

(continued)

Sylvia Little-Sweat
Wingate, NC

trace her wooden cheeks
and there
abide
inexplicably.

What is her fate but now
to wait—to wait for winter's end
and the turning of the tide?

*One of Pablo Neruda's ship masts on display in Isla Negra, Chile

***

Sally Belenardo
Branford, CT

Who's to Blame?

Who was the learned but weird man,
that quirky ornithologist
respected all throughout the land
by naturalists and scientists,
by peers acclaimed on every hand—
he, who named a handsome songbird
thus: *Turdus migratorius*?
As if we could say that without
our thinking of migrating turds.
Did Robin deserve such foul words?
I think not. Without any doubt
he chose the worst name ever heard,
and shame on the man who's to blame
for giving our Redbreast that name.

John Gillsepie
Camden, ME

hopper painting

walking down a side street
on a warm summer afternoon
your life becomes a Hopper painting

dust motes hanging in a shaft of sunlight
dance behind the plate glass windows
caressing the tchotchkes collecting dust

you are alone on the street
in a vacuum of silence,
an anonymous sadness engulfs the air
and your life has ended

or is just beginning.

***

isn't it?

the defeat is obvious

broken bits lie scattered on the floor
like diamonds in the moon light

as time melts on the edge of space
looking for a place to call home

and snow keeps falling
while death waits at the door
for your answer.

Judy O'Dell
Rockport, ME

Taking the Wrong Way Up

I paused on the mountainside to catch my breath, grateful to be healthy enough for this steep climb. There was a patch of bare rocks above me, and I scanned the terrain to figure out how to reach this next ledge. Roger had burst into the dining room of our lodge at breakfast, his hair wet. He told our group of writers about his hike to a clear blue lake at the top of the mountain, where he shed his clothes on this warm early September day and swam in the cold water. I had an immediate mental image of this lake and asked him how to get there. He told me there was a trail behind the farmhouse across the highway. After lunch, Eric, Lynn, and I walked down the gravel road to a white farmhouse and barn with a bright blue roof. We saw a sign for the parking area, pushed through waist-high Angelica behind the silo to find the broken fence, and mowed farm lane Roger had described. We followed it upward, and then it petered out. Puzzled, we looked around for another trail, did not find one, and then started to make our way upward through the brush. When we reached the first ridge, I looked down to see the tiny farmhouse and our lodge below. We must have missed the trail, but there was no way we could get lost on this treeless mountain in Iceland, so different from those I hiked in Maine. Eric and I consulted our phones to see if we could pull up Google Maps. No service. We continued to climb.

I inhaled the scent of heather and moss as I moved through the crowberry and scattered the cotton-like seedheads of Eriophorum with my pant legs. The leaves on the plants were starting to turn a vivid red. We were told Iceland had no ticks, so my only concern was a misstep between the rocks. A fall at my age could be a disaster, but I was not worried. The warm sun and bright blue sky kept me in the present, and I reached the next ridge. Above us to the east, the black lava spire of Hraundrangi gleamed in the afternoon light, and its surrounding black mountains had retained patches of snow. Lynn motioned us over to the edge of a cliff with a river running far below. I had an attack of vertigo and quickly stepped back. We surmised it was the outflow from the lake and made our way up to the next ridge. Eric was able to access Google Maps. A lake appeared on the screen. It was further to our left, but it was hard to tell how far away it was. I hiked to the next ridge, heart pumping, hoping to see water, but there was only another ridge that we could not see from below. As I looked down, the cliffs we had climbed appeared as undulating waves left by the ancient glaciers. I had never felt so small and insignificant.

Finally, at the top of the next ridge, we saw water. But it was not the clear blue lake that we expected. It was an oval gray pool in the river, but beautiful in its own way. Eric and Lynn walked down to the water while I climbed another ridge to see if the lake was there. There was only the winding river in a valley and another outlet pool glimmering in the sun. Lynn soaked her sore ankle in the cold water while Eric and I explored the riverbed. The water was clear; we could see the rocks below the surface, but no sign of aquatic life.

The afternoon light was waning, so we started back, keeping the blue roof of the farmhouse in sight. Moving diagonally down the mountain, we picked up traces of a trail that looked like the deer paths in my meadow in Maine, but there were no deer in Iceland. When we dropped below another ridge, we saw some of our group walking up, looking for us. We hiked down to meet them and noticed they were on a well-traveled trail that wound up the mountain. We had taken the wrong farm road and ended up at the outlet river instead of the lake.

I was disappointed. My mental image of the blue lake was beckoning, but it was too late in the day. I looked at the immensity around me. As is sometimes the case, the journey was just as interesting as the imagined destination.

Karen E. Wagner
Hudson, MA

Long Awaited

March is too early to say
spring in Massachusetts. Come again
in late April and I might believe you.
That tiny crocus that shows its colors now
is a snow plant
tolerant through the storms to come.

Once the weather breaks soft
and more birds sing
I'll bring myself outdoors and revel
in the air vibrant with a new season.
The wheel of the year turns to a delightful scene.

Nests, eggs, purled beings waddle
after parents. Who can resist a smile?
This end of life is so delicate
it touches even the crankiest among us.

I see fresh green, mourning doves puff
in a background of forsythia. Reminds me
my misgivings belong to yesterday, melt
with the last heaps under cinder-crusts.

I wish my life was as easy as flipping
the calendar from April to May.
Who wouldn't like to have a birthday
in May? Or carry the name
of this fair thirty-one days? May
is why I tolerate March, trudge my way
through April. True spring, no threat
of snow, winter long gone astray,
colors of puffins courting.

Dorothy Hopkins
Waldoboro, ME

Remembering Fog

Returned to her beloved Penobscot Bay,
she walks the cobbled beach drenched in salt.
She picks through broken urchins, sun-dried crabs,
through rotting kelp, debris, and storm-tossed planks.
She fingers multi-colored, tide-worn stones
and bits of pitted, luminescent glass.
Lost are all the years she's been away.
She squints into the sun, remembering fog:

Her family felt the dampness seeping through
their hair, their clothes, their pores. Her father eased
the boat through ghostly anchored yachts that wait
a fairer day to sail in open bay.
He checked his watch to set the compass course.
Crossing the reach, they blew the horn and searched—
alert for other boats, for drifting logs.
All they could see was gray on gray on gray,
a veil of mist within the boat and just
beyond, the edge where light reflected back—
nothing more, no sense of time or space.
Her father cut the engine, let them drift.
Their eyes sought any sign of tree or ledge.
They plumbed the depths to find the bar that linked
the islands where they changed their course,
but often only songs of birds on shore
revealed the islands lying there unseen
in ancient, misty world. Again they ran
for half an hour, crossed the eastern bay,
slowed, listened now for surf to break
where rolling seas would shorten near the shore.
A presence seemed to loom before the bow.
The fog thinned almost imperceptibly.

(continued)

Dorothy Hopkins
Waldoboro, ME

Moisture dripped silently from trees;
The earth was redolent with pungent scent.
Mysterious in this diminished world,
the island grew to fill their universe.

***

Sylvia Little-Sweat
Wingate, NC

Portofino Reverie

At night the lights
of Valparaiso shape into peaks
the European Hills then plunge
again to a sea
so black it could be ink
for a poet's pen.

So, too, must the blue
of the sea have been for Neruda
in Isla Negra's morning light
at his desk tracing poetry
like sea birds' tracks
before the ebbing of the tide.

From the room above
in a bed still warm with sleep
Matilde, his Eve,
woke to a murmuring sea
breaking upon black rocks
and the bluest sky since Eden.

Erik Stumpfel
Sangerville, ME

Ice Out (I)

The ice melts first along the *northern* shore,
except where freshets, brooks and streams come in.
These melt before the shores, though north or south,
and each year fools will drown in some brook's mouth
by going out on ice that's grown too thin
where snow-melt freshened springtime flows come in.

But back to northern shores: the south-sloped sun,
in gaining azimuth when the Winter's done,
will cast its rays upon the starker strand
to grow a gap twixt edge of ice and land;
show glacial dropstones, pushed as if by hand
to shallow depths, by Winter's ice now gone.

The southern shores are last to feel the sun.
Dense spruce, fir, pine and larch all screen its warmth,
to leave a half-moon, crescent, eyelid, rind
of ice, on ponds half open and half blind.

While Winter lingers on the *northern* slopes,
it also tarries on the *southern* shore;
as if to say, life *may* fulfill our hopes,
but not just yet; we have to wait some more.

From *Waiting for Spring,* unpublished poetry collection
by E. Stumpfel.

Janet Dorman
Falmouth, ME

Defrosting the Fridge

Early April in New York City. I'm standing on the 5th floor in my friend's flat, looking out the tall window that faces north to uptown Manhattan. A few blocks in that direction, in a small apartment, my brother is dying. Since he decided to stop treatment in February, I have been back and forth from Maine to offer what care and support I can. On all my trips, I have stood in this same spot, observing the same view. The practice somehow grounds me. The building is on the corner of Bleecker and Lafayette Streets, one of many former 19th century factories now converted into pricey condos in trendy NoHo, the North of Houston neighborhood.

The view never changes except for the weather and the advertising on the sides of one of the buildings. At the moment the ad is for Snapple drinks. It features four beverage bottles dressed in Village People costumes. The bottles are tilted at odd angles, suggesting a dance. I can hear them singing in my head, "It's fun to stay at the YMCA!" It's a day for staying inside somewhere.

Outside the sky is overcast; a spring snow squall blows, sending the flakes sideways. Below in pots and boxes, daffodils gamely try to remain upright. Crowds of people pour out of the corner subway entrances, scurrying about as if caught by the wind. Intent on their own purposes they spread out in individual eddies down the streets, away from each other.

Above the bustle on the street, I stand in stillness looking uptown toward Cooper Union and beyond to where my brother lives. A vibrating cellphone interrupts my stillness. The call is the expected one from my brother.

"Hey," I say, "how are you this morning?"

"I want to defrost my freezer today. When you come bring a baking pan, a bucket, a sponge, a long screwdriver and lots

Janet Dorman
Falmouth, ME

of newspapers."

My brother's apartment on East 16th Street is a tiny studio, the smallest I have ever seen. The "galley" kitchen has a sink, a two-burner stove and an under the counter fridge. On my last visit, I noticed the bulge in the freezer that prevented the door from fully closing. The only other "amenities" are a bed and a chair, squeezed into the sleeping area. The bathroom is across the hall.

"I know you have your ways of defrosting a freezer, and I have mine. We'll do it my way," he insisted.

I sigh and tentatively consider asking if it is really necessary to do this. Does it matter? My brother is in hospice care, dying of stage 4 squamous cell carcinoma.

He will likely be gone in a matter of weeks. With severely compromised lungs, the slightest task exhausts him, leaving him gasping for air. This seems to me not a good way to spend his precious time and strength, but this is his time, not mine, and so I bite back my big sister wisdom and say, "Sure, I'll be over in 30 minutes." His abrupt "thanks" ends the conversation.

I think about the thanks. Thanks for getting the stuff for me, or thanks for not offering your opinion. A bit of both I think. I know from my time as a chaplain and as a pastor, at the end of life one of the greatest gifts we can give the dying is autonomy. As their world and abilities shrink, being able to claim some semblance of a normal life, even the mundane and onerous job of defrosting a freezer counts. I know this and have counseled families on it, but I am in neither of those roles. I am the big sister about to lose her only sibling, the last of my family, and my grief comes out as impatience with him and his damn freezer. I want to extend his days as long as possible, make them comfortable, take care of him.

As I assemble the required equipment, these are the thoughts that run through my head. Locking the door behind me, I try to leave these thoughts with my imaginary self still staring out the 5th floor window above the chaotic street. I

Janet Dorman
Falmouth, ME

decide I will take my cue from the daffodils.

Shouldering the bag with the requested implements of defrosting, I forgo the subway and head up town. The twelve block walk will do me good as I need some time to formulate the next difficult conversation that has to happen—the conversation about leaving his apartment and entering a dedicated hospice facility. Rob has lived in this place for nearly fifteen years and until he got sick, I'd never been inside. He jokingly referred to it as his lair, and few were ever invited in. As small and uncomfortable as it was, this space was his fortress against the world. Terminal illness finally opened the gates.

It is a three floor walkup in a derelict building, barely meeting code, which meant the rent was cheap. That Rob gave me a key was a minor victory. Until recently, he had insisted on coming down and letting me in, until the three flights became as an ascent up the Empire State Building, sometimes taking twenty minutes as we stopped and rested for him to catch his breath. My brother would always do things his way, until he couldn't.

Entering the flat I found Rob on his bed. Before I could ask how he was doing, he directed me to start a pan of water on the stove. As we waited for the water to boil, we spoke of mundane things: the weather, my trip down from Maine, my kids. None of these conversations went very far or very deep. Just passing time.

The water finally boiled and Rob told me to pour it into the baking pan, then to put the pan in fridge. The idea was to allow the steam to melt the ice enough that it could be chipped away. Of course, the door would not close, so the steam escaped thwarting our efforts.

"This is going to take a long time," I thought to myself, but I kept my mouth shut awaiting instruction.

"Boil some more water," was his response. "I want to get this done today."

We continued in this unproductive manner, mostly in

Janet Dorman
Falmouth, ME

silence as he kept dozing off.

At some point, he realized that little progress had been made. Sitting up he demanded, "Give me the screwdriver."

Crawling out of bed, a shawl around his shoulders, he took the tool from my outstretched hand, bent over before the fridge and began chipping away at the ice. It wasn't long before he was on his knees, poking away and making little headway. Exhausted and gasping he pulled himself up, handed me the screwdriver and dropped onto the bed. I lifted his legs in aid, but he kicked me away finding a burst of energy stored in some internal battery to call upon when he needed to establish his agency. Chastened, I backed away waiting until he had his whole self on the mattress.

"I think I need some meds. Can you get the morphine?" I took the bottle from the kit left by the hospice nurse and handed it to him. He would self-administer regardless of instructions not to do so. His breathing slowed, becoming less labored and soon he was asleep. The freezer remained unconquered.

The other day when I arrived the hospice nurse was there. She was an attractive young Russian woman with whom my brother tried to flirt. As she went over his meds, he smiled slyly saying, "It's been a long time since I've done drugs with a pretty woman."

The nurse deflected in a good natured, professional manner. She brought me into the conversation explaining the dosages of morphine and Ativan, how and when they were to be administered. Rob watched bemusedly, sending me a covert wink when her head was turned. My brother was always considerate and attentive to women around him, bringing birthday bouquets to favorites. In this heart wrenching moment, I knew his flirting, his insistence on defrosting the useless fridge and climbing three flights of stairs all came from the same impetus. It was more than denial of reality, it was his need to be himself no matter what.

Janet Dorman
Falmouth, ME

This need to be in charge was going to make the conversation about a hospice facility very difficult. I was not looking forward to it, so instead I asked how he would like to proceed with the defrosting. Rob was not the only one who could dance into denial and avoidance.

Fighting off the effects of the sedatives, he told me to start more hot water and to remove the food that was languishing in the fridge: a couple of bottles of Ensure, organic plain yogurt, maybe half a dozen eggs, a container of tofu. With the exception of the Ensure all of it, in my opinion, needed to be tossed, but that was not my call. I placed the items on the counter, waiting for the water to boil. In the interim, I asked how his night had been.

"Not good," he said, "the damn machine kept beeping."

This was his oxygen machine, a necessary but unloved companion which took up an outsized amount of space in this cramped apartment. As a restless sleeper, the lines were always getting pinched, hence the beeping. I tucked that inconvenience away as a talking point on the hospice facility.

Finally, he drifted off, leaving the task to me to finish as I would, which I did. I turned the fridge off, leaving the door open allowing the heat of the stuffy room to melt the ice. I left the pan in to catch the drips. Spreading the newspapers on the floor I waited for the ice dam to loosen, then I pried it off. It clanked into the pan. Mission accomplished. I left him sleeping as I headed out.

Janet N. Gold
Camden, ME

Simplicity Pattern

In the days when mothers sewed their daughters' clothes,
a woman still lovely, weary now
but willing still to dream
of pretty party frocks and patent leather pumps,
sends her girls to bed.

It is late April,
when gold-flecked forsythia and tender-lipped forest violets
dress the spring earth.
As the sisters sleep, she lays out on the kitchen table
the Simplicity pattern's tissue promise of carefully stitched
shirtwaists.
Her hands hold the pinking shears
and with each cut a third-grader's surprise
becomes delight as she tries on
the white-and-yellow checked dress,
full-skirted, matching belt,
rickrack at the neck and trim for the cap sleeves.
The older sister steps into the violet dress,
fashioned as a fifth-grader's princess raiment
and down the road they walk,
almost too elated to notice
the fast-flowing brook tumbling over rocks,
the robins and finches whistling to them
as Newfield Road merges with Main Street
and they see the red brick school
and the children on the playground
and the yellow and purple of their full skirts
swirl with the fresh new air of May.

Janet N. Gold
Camden, ME

Did we tell her we cherished her hands
that cut and fit and stitched the colors of spring;
her pride, that sent us off in new dresses
to dance around the Maypole;
her gifts, more than I can count
or even remember?

It was in the days when love was spoken
in the tissue rustle of a Simplicity pattern,
in the careful choice of purple cotton and yellow and white
checks,

the unnecessary expense of rickrack to make the dress
special,
the matching fabric-covered belt to cinch the small waists
and add an extra flare
to the dancing skirts of the daughters' new dresses.

***

Steve Troyanovich
Florence, NJ

whispers of light

for Osip Mandelstam

groping the traces
of wounded light
tomorrow disappears...
a star whispers
its meaning

Julie Babb
Damariscotta, ME

Joseph

How can I not believe her?
Her eyes, filled with wonder, tears of fear,
Brimming with surprise and truth—
How can I not believe her?
She is to be my wife, she
But herself a child—too small
To bear such a weight,
Yet chosen to bear a Child
Not of my making; yet
Foretold by angels and prophets!
How can I not believe her?
She stands before me, erect, proud,
No shame, no sorrow. Undefiled.
How can I not believe her?
So I, although no more than a carpenter,
A man of faith with no earthly goods
To bestow upon either mother or Child,
Embark on this terrifying journey
With my love, my Mary, my intended.
Whose belly swells with sweet mystery,
Whose heart swells with expectant joy—
How can I not believe her?

Helen Ackermann
Rothschild, WI

What Can We Learn From Baseball?

Grandparents often spend time watching their grandchildren play various sports. Time permitting, they attend baseball games, football games, basketball games, and other sporting events. We have fallen into the group who watches baseball.

At first watching the game was simply that, watching, but not being that involved. We simply enjoyed seeing our grandsons play. The intricacies of the game were pretty much ignored. As time went on, however, I learned that any sport is much more complicated than first meets the eye.

First of all, there are many people involved. The game involves a number of coaches, athletic trainers, umpires, managers, ground keepers and others. All work together to make the game happen. We watch college baseball as well as high school baseball. I discovered that there are other elements to the game. Soon I began to care not only about our grandsons' involvement but also that of the entire team. I cheered for the entire team. Our grandsons taught us the importance of that.

They showed us what it meant to be a team player. If another person on the team had a difficult time, they were compassionate. If a team player was successful, they were happy for him. Thinking only of yourself is not the way of the game. Thinking of the entire team is what is important.

As I came to realize the intricacies of the game, I was able to apply those intricacies to our society. Why can't we care about our entire team, our society? Why can't we be concerned about the common good? What is good for all of us? Some people might be having difficulty because of various challenges; we need to realize that they need our support. Each member of society needs to be treated with respect if they are to contribute to the whole. Each needs to be

Helen Ackermann
Rothschild, WI

encouraged and given assistance when he or she needs it.

Recognizing what baseball is really about helped me to recognize the importance of looking at our society differently. Living in society demands care and concern for all the members and finding ways to support each person. We are part of a team.

***

Peggy Trojan
Brule, WI

Raspberry Jam

My teenage grandson asked me
to teach him how to make jam.
I handed him a pail,
to pick five inches of berries
from my garden.

He followed my directions,
getting his equipment ready,
measuring sugar and berries,
and cooking.
Filled his jars and sealed them.

"Good job! When they are cool,
you can label them," I said,
thinking type and date, like mine.

He wrote, on every lid,
"Alec's jam. Do not touch."

Cordula Mathias
Trevett, ME

What Would Jonah Say?

When the belly of the whale
is filled with plastic
will we change our way?

When yet more school children
get a belly full of bullets:
will we find our way?

What is needed to
get beyond the
reflexive “Nay”

Where we seek a “Yea”
to collaboration for
a peaceful way?

Who will lead the way
for common-sense
to hold sway?

Gerald George
Belfast, ME

Alas the King

She was so tender in her innocence,
lovely as a lilac, just sixteen!
Thus thought the king as he released the door
of the sumptuous carriage that brought her over the border.
Their marriage would bring together (O happy day!)
the power of her father's house with his
in close alliance. Who would ever imagine
so fragile a flower, offspring of that old dolt.
And I, he mused, how could I have such luck,
born into royalty, handsome, exceedingly rich,
and now, this queen—"Come out and marry me!"
The maid stayed put, spat right in his eye.

Well, the deal was done; he couldn't renege.
So back to his castle he took the lamentable lass,
gave her a room of her own with ladies in waiting,
and all the accoutrements of comfort.
Maybe, he surmised, she could be induced
from her high dudgeon, learn at last to love
the man who offered her a queenly crown
if she'd but share with him the royal bed.
She let her ladies in, the servants too.
But when he came to knock upon her door,
she shouted out most odious abuse:
"I'd much prefer a nunnery! Get gone!"

Soon after came a frantic messenger.
The king next door, his father-in-law-to-be,
called upon him urgently to fulfill
the vow he'd made, come aid him in a fight
against a mighty force invading now.

(continued)

Gerald George
Belfast, ME

So, of course, he called up his militant men,
took off at break-neck speed to reach the field
whereon the forces of his father-in-law
were barely hanging on. Dear God, the fray!
It lasted for eight days until at last
the invader, vanquished, quick-retreated home.
She'd have him now—the hero of the war!

Ah, the wonder of it, how in this life
strange things occur, for as he fought afar,
his own home castle came under fierce attack.
Alas, alack, an enemy had waited
till he'd gone off, then struck, took territory,
and stood before his gates, intending to enter.
But lo—up on a balcony, an incorporeal
bit of a wisp—the girl!—raised high a sword,
urged the palace guard to remain in place,
holding the gates, then heat great vats of pitch
to hurl on the heads of the enemy. 'Midst the din
they heard her shout out cries of encouragement.

How they responded! The great gates stayed firm,
flying pitch came down upon the foe,
kept them in confusion until, at last,
the king came home. He took one look,
then routed the lot, sent them fleeing in grief.
He waved to the girl—"My love, I'm coming up!"
Releasing his horse, he bounded over the stairs,
found the brave lady, exhausted, nearly collapsed.
"My dear, you've saved my castle. Be my queen!"
Her eyes flashed flame. "You pitiful stupid fool!
I fought only for this: to be left alone.
Please—some nunnery—now—I want to go!"

Margaret Roncone
Vashon, WA

Clock Tick

I grow older as my name does
Eight letters too long
for a skinny girl of nine years—
my eyes shut waiting
for the next letter to arrive.
Father always needed
space between fork and
necessary knife
Mother stirring at the stove
while the pot swallowed
unspoken words.
Sometimes organs fail
and the brain
hands out cue cards
to confuse us.
I shoved them in
my back pocket bulging
at the mouth of day.

***

Sally Belenardo
Branford, CT

Concert in Roma

The pianist said,
as he began to play, "It's
sonata easy!"

Alan White
Kailua, HI

Returning Home Can Be Bittersweet...

Home is usually where we want to end up when we retire and reach an age when travel and exploration is less appealing—but is this always true? My family and I just returned from living and working in Indonesia—a great experience and a culmination of a career of working in southeast Asia. But returning "home" made us realize that home can become elusive when one is accustomed to living and working with a diversity of people and cultures that are different from one's upbringing. In other words, the life away and its dimensions, plus the expanded understanding about what makes up our world from overseas life experiences, can change us. This missive hails from our family's recent tenure in Indonesia but first a bit of history to set the stage.

I joined the Peace Corps in the 1970s after university and found myself in Ecuador and Galapagos Islands for almost seven years. Coming home I went back to school but could not temper my curiosity to explore other parts of the world and pursue a career in environmental conservation in developing countries.

This led me to the Philippines, doing research on marine resource issues, finding full time employment and my wonderful wife. Our adventures then led us back to U.S., to Sri Lanka for several years, back to Philippines and then our home in Hawaii. But not to leave new stones unturned we took on what purported to be a difficult assignment in Indonesia even though well into social security age.

Living in Indonesia from 2016 until 2021 felt like a whole new life of unimagined complexities, language, magnitude of geographic size and distances, mixing of people and friendships. Although difficult at times, it proved to be a new world of learning and building respect for a place and people that is little understood by those not fortunate enough to be

Alan White
Kailua, HI

immersed in the place and its culture. It turned out to be an enjoyable experience and was the right decision, but we didn't realize its potential to change us and our view of the world.

Our home in Jakarta, a city of almost 12 million people, may not sound ideal to many, but surprisingly it grew on us because the city does not fulfill the negative connotations associated with many large cities. It is rather a friendly place, there is little serious crime and no matter where you shop or transact business, people are courteous and are not offended by outsiders or different ethnicities in their presence. The stereotypes that can permeate our perceptions of large cities in the U.S. were largely absent to our surprise. Being a Muslim majority country and the first time for us to live in a mostly Islamic culture triggered some uncertainty in the beginning but this disappeared after a few months in the country reminding us how misleading are the images and messages we often hear and internalize from our media at home.

Working closely with many young, aspiring and caring Indonesians was a truly profound experience in that it came to feel like home for my wife and I. She immersed herself with an orphanage that had a swimming pool as part of an old colonial style home that was turned into a residence and school for young people without supporting families. What a thrill it was to see the boys and girls take up swimming even while wearing their body covering swim attire. The group of kids also showed interest in learning ukulele, a favorite of my wife, leading to a concert performed in the American Club as a fund raiser for the school. In my office with about 50 Indonesian staff, I experienced comradery in ways not experienced before and also to my surprise, the mix of Christian and Muslim faiths never posed issues since all always greeted the others religious holidays, be they birth of Muhammed, Jesus or Buddha, etc. And to liven up the office atmosphere, lunch time one day a month was set aside to celebrate birthdays meaning that there were lots of lively meals and too much food since the custom is for the birthday celebrant to provide snacks. And, Indonesian cuisine is very tasty once one gets used to the spices that might pose an obstacle to some. But a fond memory is the humor present as people loved to poke fun at each other for mostly not offensive laughs and funny WhatApp cartoons.

COVID brought difficult times in Jakarta, as all over the world, as the virus spread and government mandated a series of lockdowns with various levels of travel restrictions and office attendance limitations. But, despite the pain of the pandemic and knowing some friends and their family who were directly affected, our project team carried on using Zoom and Teams calls on a daily basis for both business and social interactions and our office stayed open with a skeleton crew following rotations on who could be present. Many preferred being in the office to get out of their often small homes busy with children or other distractions. Also, as elsewhere office staff complained about a lack of social contact by only staying at home. It was a bit different from the work from home trends and discussions we now see. A joke about how Indonesia would handle the pandemic at the peak in 2020 that circulated was: "China curbed the spread through discipline; the U.S. lost control through ignorance; India turned into a disaster because of religion; and here we are in Indonesia with no discipline, being ignorant and having too much religion—what will happen?" Such humor was not uncommon and being a democratic country with a relatively free press, editorials do not mince words when targeting some governance and corruption issues in the country. In fact, the daily *Jakarta Post* is considered a breath of fresh air for journalism in Southeast Asia. And in hindsight, Indonesia has done somewhat better than several of its northern neighbors Covid wise!

Our last year in Jakarta being pandemic kept us close to our condominium complex that fortunately had amenities

Alan White
Kailua, HI

and great neighbors. We had not really gotten to know our neighbors prior to the pandemic and as a result of people staying home, a new community of friends emerged that would not have happened without the lockdowns. We managed a few outdoor pot luck dinners, birthdays and getting to know kids as we played at poolside—special times in hindsight even though all bemoaned the situation which in reality was not bad compared to many places.

As our time in Indonesia drew to a close in 2021, our desire to return home was not as strong as we would have anticipated five years earlier. We hadn't realized how much we had adapted to the lifestyle, the culture, and how many close friends we had made both through work and social gatherings where we lived. Our office team had become more like an extended family and until this day we have active WhatsAp messages and calls to stay in touch. An office party ensued as lockdowns eased and our neighbors held a special gathering where all told stories about times together, the good food shared, the games played and how our discussions would be missed. Men friends in our condo always gathered each afternoon to discuss the U.S. election in late 2020 and of course they asked many questions about why the election was so contentious. These discussions reminded me how much people in developing countries look to the U.S. as a model of democracy and become truly worried when it appears to be in trouble. Again, these discussions made us a bit apprehensive about returning "home" because we really enjoyed the openness of people's concerns and how several of our neighbors regularly brought us great Indonesian food to boot!

After almost 40 years of living and working mostly in Southeast Asia and having returned home on various occasions, it is never as easy and attractive as we might expect. It is difficult to leave and say good bye and equally difficult once home because we are out of touch with old friends and often friends and family cannot relate to where we came from

Alan White
Kailua, HI

and what is in our minds and hearts. It takes time to readjust and there is real truth to the adage, that reverse culture shock can be the most difficult. When returning from Ecuador in the 1970s to life at home I still remember trying to figure out how I would fit back in and thus went back to school—a common response of younger people. Now at retirement age I realize that my desire to travel, learn and be challenged was always in me so I ended up going out yet again (and again). But I have never regretted all the wonderful adventures and people I have worked with in foreign lands and even though the return home is difficult and quite bittersweet, such is the life that some of us have chosen with no regrets!

***

Robert B. Moreland
Pleasant Prairie, WI

Miles From Minot

Amber prairie grass bows before
west zephyrs, undulating sea.
Horizon endless, range adore,
just my dappled grey mare and me.

Some would fear this rare solitude,
breathing matching kiss of the wind...
High in the saddle, stretch, gaze shrewd;
God's paintbrush, beginning to end.

Burning daylight with miles to go,
small ranch house warm awaits beyond.
Sun caressed black hills, touched with snow,
whisper to my horse, she responds.

Emily Blair Stribling
Brooklin, ME

No Trace

The field out back is mowed.
Potatoes, garlic and onions cured,
pesto and tomato sauce stored,
and the last to be harvested
winter squash on its cellar shelf.
In the garden only solitary stalks
of kale and chard remain.

Tomorrow we will put away
the porch furniture,
snap in storm windows, coil hoses,
stack the last of the wood.
Hay is in the barn, the water pipe taped.
In the paddock only goldenrod
retain their color.

We have removed all traces of summer
as if we had never floated
on the smooth surface of its
pond of light, and let
time go its own way,
as if we had never lingered
to watch falling stars
dapple the shores of night,

as if we had never grilled
fresh cod,
as if the fading light hadn't haloed
our visiting children,
telling each other the stories
of their grownup lives,
as if we had never played croquet
or sailed past Pumpkin Light.

Emily Blair Stribling
Brooklin, ME

Like a dream we don't remember,
summer slips away from us,
pale filaments swirling
in the gold flecked air of autumn,
only a final blue burst
of blue hydrangea,
and the eternity of sea and sky.

***

P. C. Moorehead
North Lake, WI

Healing

The cat meowed,
and I hated her.
She purred,
and I hated her more.

"Leave me alone;
I want to die."
Purr—
"Leave me alone."
Meow—
"Leave me alone."

Well, maybe I can pet you.
I stretch out my hand.
She noses me—
"Purr," I say.

Patrick T. Randolph
Lincoln, NE

Westbound Winter Train

Train moves across winter fields;
When it inhales and releases its breath,
Puffs of white phantoms linger in the air—
Homeless spirits looking for love.

Snow starts to fall;
The train disappears in its own breath—

A conductor stares out the midnight window—
Smiles at a village of curious ghosts.

***

Waiting

Train station—ancient man's sigh;
Gnarled fingers interwoven.

His momentary thoughts—
Crowded memories;
Faces of old friends.

Margie Thumm
Raymond, ME

Owning My Tenacity

Tenacity: persistence, perseverance, stubbornness, stamina, determination, endurance, obstinacy, spunk, grit, spirit, courage, woman.... These words are on the back of my "Tenacity" mug.

Tenacious female. Born 1945. Raised in Ohio.

It's been a challenging road for me to travel. Now, in my seventies, I am very glad to have that "perseverance gene." It has served me well, but man-oh-man/woman-oh-woman, it's not been easy. If I had been born in the 1800's, I figure I would have been one of the women on the wagon trains heading West. They had grit, at least the ones who survived and kept going.

I say "perseverance gene" because of my paternal ancestors. My father's mother entered law school in 1917. Though she never finished, she none-the-less entered this male dominated realm. She was a single mom. Her sister made a bundle of money through her stock market investments even with the Market Crash of 1928 and ensuing Depression. Her money supported not only her, but also her husband and his second wife, long after she had died. When Dad said that my determination would keep me single, I wanted to point out to him that I came by my independence honestly...from his genes...and why would that keep me single? He expected me to go to college and do well in school, so what was the problem with speaking up?

My mother was quietly independent and an example to me. She related a story about Dad giving her envelopes to help manage the household finances. This system was rejected. Dad later commented that she had good instinct for running a home, including the money side of things. Mom drove her Willy's Jeepster in the Labor Day parade filled with the girls in my Brownie Scout troop that she led. She made all the sloppy joes for the Woodside School Fall Festival, leading the booth and that project. She was part of a group that helped establish kindergarten as part of the public school system in our hometown. Once I commented on a roster of a women's group that listed the members by their husbands' names. "Mom, how do they know what YOUR name is?" Apparently, she brought this up to the group. She proudly showed me the next publicized list: it had their first names, with their husbands' names in parentheses (telephone listings were in the men's names at the time–the 1960s).

It has taken me years to grow into this mantel of persistence and own it as my own. I am now pleased about my resilience and endurance, even with what life has thrown at me. A couple of events solidified for me that tenacity was a positive attribute to have and it was mine to embrace as I chose.

One was a special exhibit I viewed in March 2019 at The Jamestown Settlement Museum in Jamestown, Virginia. The exhibit was entitled, "Tenacity." It was about the women in Jamestown and Early Virginia that came to help settle the New World. Though seldom mentioned in history, their contribution was vital to the development of the colonies. I bought mugs for myself, my daughter, daughter-in-law, and stepdaughters with the "TENACITY" logo of the exhibit on one side and the definition of tenacity on the other. Later I ordered a dozen mugs to give to my tenacious women friends.

Another thought-provoking exhibit was at the Maine State Museum in Augusta which I visited in May 2019. It was about the 100 years before women got the right to vote. There were many outstanding, determined women who worked tirelessly on this issue. Because they were outspoken, they were ostracized for their beliefs and work. No mugs to purchase there, but the message of tenacity spoke to me.

My spunk has helped me: as I learned to ride a two-wheeler; completed my senior year of high school at a new school; get off probation in college and graduate on schedule;

Margie Thumm
Raymond, ME

complete graduate school, paying for it myself; raise two children; complete a challenging nurse practitioner course at almost fifty; go through a divorce and buy a house.... The list goes on.

Tenacious female. Born 1945. Resident of Maine. Still tenacious AND finally embracing it.

***

Peggy Trojan
Brule, WI

Sharing an Order

Waitresses often
think it quaint
that Dave and I share orders,
not understanding
we have done this for thirty years
in an effort to limit
our waistlines.
We remind them to bring
only one roll,
often can't finish our half
of the meal.
Once we ordered one piece of pie
after dinner and the waitress
proudly severed it
with two forks,
surrounded by a heart
of whipped cream.

Sally Belenardo
Branford, CT

Road Kill

The traffic rushes by its slaughtered prey.
An animal that left its burrow dies.
Crows try to stab its flesh, and hop away.

No one had meant to injure it or slay,
yet wind-blown fur on bloodstained asphalt lies,
where speeding cars rush by their slaughtered prey.

The scavengers may glean a meal today
if they are cautious in approach, and wise,
avoid the rushing cars, and flit away.

They pace the highway's shoulder, there they stay,
aware they could, as well, meet their demise
where speeding cars surround their slaughtered prey.

The crows attempt to pounce and pierce and flay.
Each with another for a portion vies;
they tear off scraps of flesh and lift away.

The corpse, if not devoured, will decay;
its starving young emit unanswered cries.
The traffic soon obliterates its prey.
The crows snatch bits of flesh and fly away.

***

On a Hill in April

White cloud beyond
it, quickly a bare oak becomes
a pear tree in bloom.

Genie Dailey
Jefferson, ME

It's Maine

Harbingers of spring—
budding trees, early robins,
and it's mud season

***

Maine Spring

Twisted, wintry limbs
Reach out for springtime sunshine—
Soon, apple blossoms

***

Look West

Wild pallet colors,
Orange, purple, and slate blue—
Late August sunset

E. M. Barsalou
Dover, NH

Through the Grove

Down the old-logging road,
One not taken in many moons.
Off the side of a beaten track,
Made by the feet of animal and man.
Tempered through a long time by the trail,
You make good time;
Follow it in, it covers and regains within
Full forests hood. Domain of the woods.
Tracking past through alders and pines,
Winding along the wooded spine of ascent.
Takes you back to a place called home,
Where you walked as a child; no one even drove.
A calming space to ease your mind,
Down beneath the wood-line.
In the slithy toves, walking in through the grove.

"The creation of a thousand forests is in one acorn."
—Ralph Waldo Emerson

Alfred Kildow
Boothbay Harbor, ME

TV Tots

They met at Toohey's every afternoon at five. That's when it opened. Lee and Mike would quaff a few or three with their friend Dewey, the bartender. He called them his regular regulars.

Lee and Mike were artists. Dewey, with three toddlers at home with his wife, delighted in listening to the outrageous stories the duo told, playing off each other, inventing scenarios that addled Dewey's brain.

"When did you first start drawing?" Lee asked Mike one afternoon.

"I think I was about three. Started drawing cartoons. Probably copying stuff I saw in the Sunday paper."

"Me, too," Lee replied. "I remember drawing cartoons all the way through.... Heck, I still draw them. Mostly as doodles when my serious painting droops."

Both Lee and Mike were well-known serious artists, at least in their town and in their small social circles. Lee painted portraits, on commission; Mike crafted imaginative landscapes. Neither made much money. Both had wives who worked. Neither raised children, although Mike had a long-estranged teenaged son who lived with his first wife.

***

"I have an idea," Mike said one afternoon as he slipped onto his customary stool at the bar and gripped the pint that sat there waiting for him. "It just came to me, walking in the door just now. Crazy idea."

He spun it out for his companions: A TV show. For children. By children. Except, Mike and Lee would pose as children in a half-hour play that would lean heavily on drawing. Comics. For children, by children. The artist duo would do the drawing, right on the set, and do all of the dialog themselves. They'd even draw likenesses of their juvenile selves to wear as face coverings.

"So, this seems like a lot of work," Lee said. "Writing scripts, drawing comic strips, preparations for filming. No way."

Mike picked up his pint, sipped, then drank. "You got it all wrong, Lee. We'll do it live. Wing it. How hard can it be to pretend to be a three-year-old, draw like a three-year-old, talk like a.... Well, maybe a five-year-old."

They wrestled with the idea for several days. Dewey became an enthusiastic booster, imagining how his three under-five-youngsters would react to such a program. As the idea persisted in their conversations, albeit only after the first pint was long gone, Lee and Mike found themselves with a maturing idea. Dewey provided the link: "My cousin is the program director at WGWZ. I'll talk to him."

Two weeks later, *Drawn-Out Adventures* hit TV screens in the town for the first time. At 7 am on a Sunday morning.

News of the upcoming show had spread quickly by word of mouth among the dozen or so close friends of the artists. The station didn't plan to sample viewership. On Sunday mornings the station came on the air at 6 am with a recorded sermon from the pastor of the First Baptist Church. Presumably, a few churchgoers would hang around to watch the debut of DOA.

On Monday, promptly at five, Lee and Mike grasped their pints and waited for Dewey's comments. They came quickly, enthusiastically and expansively.

"My kids were over the moon," Dewey exclaimed. "When you were drawing those faces, they drew right along with you. When you told those crazy stories, they laughed, danced and made up little stories of their own. You're a hit. At least in my house."

A short note in the TV section of the local paper promised to advance viewership the next week. And so it went. Despite the early Sunday morning time slot, parents with early-rising young children tuned in, drawing materials at the ready.

Six months later, *Drawn-Out Adventures* moved to a new time slot, 4 pm weekdays, five days a week.

Their die was cast for them. Lee and Mike now had regular jobs. Lee proposed they meet mornings to plan each afternoon's show, and perhaps make preliminary plans for upcoming shows.

"Naw, no way. We wing it," Mike insisted. And they did.

Sometimes Lee would suggest something a few minutes before airtime, but he soon realized that Mike wasn't listening. When the director wagged his finger to start the show, Mike would swirl a few lines from a black crayon on a sheet of drawing paper, don the drawing as a mask—and start talking. After a minute or so of scene-setting childish rhetoric describing a madcap adventure featuring two small boys, Lee would pick up the thrust of Mike's latest and play right along. The action was illustrated with on-the-spot instant drawings.

Their show soon became a booming success. Not only did it capture nearly all of the three to five year olds in the town, but many older children tuned in as well, revisiting their carefree pasts. And the usually conservative Lee fully embraced Mike's "wing it" attitude. "It's really a lot of fun," he admitted one day. "I'm a kid again. Every afternoon at four."

***

Their success in attracting viewers also attracted top ratings and favorable mentions in newspapers throughout the region. Others noticed as well.

The station director asked them to come in for a meeting on Saturday morning. "Some guys from network headquarters in New York will be visiting and they asked to meet with you."

Lee was nervous, unsuccessfully trying to learn why the

meeting was scheduled, what would be discussed, what questions might be asked.

Mike's reaction: "Hey, it's not until after noon. We'll both be awake by then. We'll dazzle them with our fancy footwork."

Neither they, nor the station director who was seated in neutral territory at the head of the table could have anticipated what was to follow. Three executives from the network, each wearing double-breasted blue suits, vests and flamboyant neckties, sat across a conference room table from the casually-clad Lee and Mike. The three executives, stony-faced, spoke seriously and rapidly: "Your afternoon show is getting rave reviews," one said. "It's the top-rated daytime program in this area."

Lee beamed; Mike sat dead-panned, not responding. Suspicious. Saw "The Suits" as a threat.

"And that is why," the leader of The Suits proclaimed, "we are taking this show national. Prime spot on the network. Putting it at the top of the heap, as it were, for our daytime programming. Internal polling shows that we should always try to attract children at an early age to make them become enduring viewers. And that is why...."

Mike was no longer listening. He was certain he could foretell what was about to come. Lee continued to smile broadly, nodding in agreement as the leader of The Suits went on.

"Naturally, as a network, we can't continue with the spontaneity of the program as currently constituted. We will film each program in advance. In fact, we have already filmed 15 episodes and are hard at work on more."

Lee's smile began to fade. "But I haven't..." he began before the Lead Suit interrupted him.

"We also think it unwise to have adult males pose as children, so we have cast a number of small children to pose as artists and others to tell stories, although an adult, a woman, a school-teacher sort, is leading the stories.

"We liked the pilot and the next two episodes so much we've given the green light to the entire series. It airs starting Monday at four."

Lee cleared his throat. "So, what about us? I mean, it's our show, right?"

Mike smiled knowingly, said nothing.

"Well, technically it's not your show," Lead Suit said quietly. "Our station director here quite responsibly signed you to a contract that spelled out in clear legal terms...."

***

On Monday afternoon at 5 o'clock the WGWZ switchboard lit up and the call forwarding recording worked overtime. The callers were angry.

At Toohey's, Dewey arrived a few minutes early, stood perched behind the bar, waiting. Even before drawing pints for his friends, he erupted angrily. "What in the world have you done? Your show isn't worth (exclamation deleted). Two of my kids walked away almost immediately and the little one began crying."

By week's end, the station, overwhelmed, stopped answering the phones. At the network, executives ignored the feedback, awaiting viewership numbers and ratings.

Numbers and ratings dropped through the floor.

The Suits persisted and the show, which had been renamed "Tot Drawers," continued for another six weeks. While The Suits ignored the results, someone was watching. Someone from the network's board of directors. A memorandum came hurtling down on The Suits:

"Bring back the original show, *Drawn-Out Adventures*. Bring back the original stars, Mitch, Lou, whatever their names are. Get them back on the air. Now."

***

Alfred Kildow
Boothbay Harbor, ME

Dewey pushed two pints across the bar as his friends eased onto their stools. “So, what’s the plan? You going back on the air? Gonna be TV stars again.”

Lee looked at his stein while Mike took a long slug. “Nope, not a chance,” Mike said. “They stole our idea, (exclamation deleted) it up and there’s no way I’m gonna rescue them.”

Dewey placed both hands on the bar, fingers spread. “My kids are so disappointed. They really miss the show. I’ll betcha that’s a universal feeling across kid-dom.”

There was a long silence while the artists sipped. Dewey poured one for himself.

“I have an idea,” Mike said. The others turned to face him, listening carefully.

“We’ll do it live,” he said in a quiet voice. “Just for the neighborhood. Probably can book the elementary school auditorium. Do the show for two hours, live, with an audience of kids. Let the little ones roam the place, come up on stage and help us draw. Invent stories with us. Keep it small.”

Lee laughed. “And in our control. Completely. Without a contract.”

“I’ll drink to that,” Dewey said, raised a hand and the three friends clapped their hands together cheerfully.

Jean Biegun
Davis, CA

Winter Invitation

When you go
where snowshoes are needed
where no trail guides the way,
silence in great soft white robes
slowly leads
where mysteries lay.

Deep wing imprints
left with fur tufts invite you
to read snow,
conjure stories
of a Cooper's Hawk sweep
powerful and low.

Zigzag rabbit tracks gallop
to dense shrubs, here a fox
ran on pads thick and wide,
a fur pellet of bones
drops by a tree where
Great Horned Owls might hide.

When the goldenrod galls nod
mutely to close the long
snowshoes day,
cool flakes whisper gently near
your flushed checks: *Come back,*
whenever you may.

Thomas Peter Bennett
Silver Spring, MD

Audubon's Caracara Eagle

"Until my visit to the Floridas,"
        Audubon wrote,
        "I was not aware of
The Caracara or Brazilian Eagle
        in the United States.

Near St. Augustine, I observed
        a bird flying at a great elevation.
Unknown to me, and bent on obtaining it,
        I followed nearly a mile . . .
and saw it sail for the earth.

The bird landed on a dead horse,
        where turkey buzzards and
carrion crows were feeding
        on the savory carcass.

I crawled along a deep ditch,
        pushing my gun before me,
making occasional observations
        of my intended prey.

Getting as close as I could,
        I was still wary of a sure shot . . .
raised up, shot, and missed . . . shot again,
as the bird flew away.
Two days later,
        I dispatched my assistant,
who returned with the bird
        in less than an hour.

Thomas Peter Bennett
Silver Spring, MD

*I immediately began my drawing and
upon completion, made a
double drawing for the purpose of
showing all its feathers."*

***

Peggy Trojan
Brule, WI

Coinage, 1940's

We called them lead pennies,
but really they were steel
coated with zinc.
All the copper was needed
for the war.
No count was kept of the steel coins made,
but only forty copper pennies
remain from 1943.
We didn't care much.
A penny was a penny,
good for a choice
from the candy counter
in Webster's store.

Sister Irene Zimmerman
Greenfield, WI

Keys

A month ago, when you phoned me
to say you had lost the key to your house,
I came and retrieved the extra one
from the hiding place you had shown me
before you left for vacation.
You laughed, embarrassed, and thanked me.

Today I stopped by and found you knocking
at your door. *But this is your own house,*
I told you. *No one else lives here.*
I retrieved the hidden key again
and unlocked the door for you.
You thanked me and asked my name.

Dear friend, I wish I could find
a hidden key to your mind
so that I could unlock that door for you
and you could come home.

Skip Simonds
Boothbay, ME

The Last Goodby

As he lay in the bed with his wife of more than 40 years, she was sleeping peacefully and his thoughts returned as they often did, to that night 50 years ago when his heart had been broken when his first and most intense relationship ended. He didn't always go back to that night with thoughts of her, but of late it was more and more often. He wondered what his life would have been like had that first love stayed, had she not run off without explanation.

He was happy with his life, his marriage, his family, all of it. But he was dogged by the "what if" that haunted the back corridors of his mind in the quiet of the night. Somehow, as good as it all was, he believed deep down in that place he never acknowledged out loud that life would have been better with his first love.

He knew such thoughts robbed him of the ability to fully let go in the relationships he now had. They were speed bumps, potholes, and impediments to fully loving his wife and family. He hated it, but he felt trapped. How does anyone resolve those things? One cannot.

His wife was breathing deeply...she never snored...that was a mystery in itself. She had tried to stay awake as he had, but had drifted off in the quiet of that balmy summer evening. They were waiting for the comet. Unlike others in history, this one was passing so close to Earth that it was only going to be visible in the sky as a comet with a tail...that classic comet...for that one night.

For two weeks before it had been a slowly growing, brightening dot of light in the sky, the tail hidden behind it as it approached. For the two weeks following its transit of the sky, it would become its opposite: a slowly diminishing, dimming dot of light that was actually the tail obscuring the comet, eventually to be lost in the glare of the sun.

Skip Simonds
Boothbay, ME

But tonight was the big show. They said it would be like being a hitch-hiker standing on the side a desert road. You would see the truck coming up and over the horizon in the distance, almost not moving, but growing in intensity as it got nearer and nearer. Then in a flash it would be upon you and go by with wind and dust and noise and commotion, mussing up your hair, causing you to squint and blink, involuntarily taking a step back from the road.

And then it would recede to eventually disappear noiselessly over the other horizon.

As he lingered with the bittersweet thought of first love, lost love, the comet transformed from that large dot to its full display. The bedroom became as bright as noonday. He had not expected such an awe-inducing event. He was lost in the light. Everything disappeared in the blindness of brightness. There was a smell of ozone, an almost wizardly odor, like the passing of the most intense thunderstorm you could imagine.

The light lasted for the better part of an hour, although he wasn't aware of it. To him it was like a flash. Slowly the blindness that follows bright lights faded and he found himself in a strange bedroom. No, he realized, it was eerily familiar. It was his college apartment.

He heard the steady breathing beside him and figured somehow his wife had been brought there with him. But it was not his wife. It was her. He got up, quietly, so as not to disturb her and went to the bathroom, closed the door, and turned on the light. It was his face that greeted him in the mirror, but a face where somehow time had been erased or turned back.

His world was totally inverted. He was young again. He was with her again. And yet he had the accumulated memories of what he guessed was going to be the next 50 years.

Somehow he had gone back in time. He was sure it was fifty years ago to the day he had been alone in his bed when the comet passed over and he found himself no longer 71 but

Skip Simonds
Boothbay, ME

21 and exactly where he was at age 21: in her arms.

His memory was intact. He knew his history. He knew he'd lived those 50 years in real time, that she had broken his heart, that he had married someone else, had children, pursued a career, several careers in fact. But it had all been without her.

That night, fifty years ago, had been bliss. The next morning...and he never knew why...she had left him. There had been no rational reason, no labored explanation, no "long good-by." She just left and never came back.

Oh, they talked by phone after that fateful night, at least as much as she was willing to talk, which wasn't much. But it was clear, oh so painfully clear, that she was never coming back. It took years to get his balance back, the loss was so jarring.

And then, after 50 years, the comet came and took him back to that very night.

He gently woke her. He told her of his life without her, told her of it all, and she understood it.

The next morning she did not leave, and he lived another whole life, this time with her.

And now, that same 50 years had passed again...this time with her...initially in bliss. But he carried the memories of the imperfect life he had lived without her, with another woman as his wife and partner, the kids that he knew had existed but now were never to be born.

The cumulative weight of what was not to be fell on him incrementally, but unceasingly as the years went by. There was joy with her, and a richness that he had not known in the other life. But it was not enough to counter the impact of what was never to be.

He felt selfish. He felt that he was cheating on his other wife and family, even though they did not, could not exist in this timeline. There was no one to feel that they were being cheated on, but regardless the feeling persisted in his heart.

Eventually, the bliss turned to something less white hot.

Skip Simonds
Boothbay, ME

As the years progressed, he was never angry or upset with her. It was not her fault. He perhaps knew it was his desire that had been the raw material the comet had turned into the substance of the life he was now living.

Is there a force more indelible on a person's heart than unrequited love? Does anyone ever find the salve that cleans and heals that hurt? Does forgetfulness ever serve as such? Or does it merely hide the hurt, fooling you into thinking it is in the past, until the reflection of some sunbeam upon rippled water unexpectedly recalls it, and it floods your heart again?

Now, it was the night of the comet again. His life had come full circle, this time according to his desires. She was asleep, breathing deeply, unable to stay awake.

As she lay on her back in the dark save the light of a waning moon through the window, the woman she was 50 years ago appeared in her face. Lines of age disappeared. Skin, smoothed and stretched loverly across her features. She was as she was so long ago. The ethereal glow of her emergent youth caused the darkness to frame her face like a somber vignetting. She was a living picture of herself from their first love.

He woke her. He was instantly stilled as his face hovered above hers. The glow captured him. This resurfacing of the love of his youth slew him. He was a dead man, killed by a love beyond his capacity to hold within him...burst asunder...as he fell headlong into the softness of that dream come true.

But the eyes. The eyes became both young and old at the same time and he realized they were that way then as well...remembering back as though it was earlier today. Perhaps it was.

Her face was the ghost of her youth risen to life, filled, animated, sad beyond belief, glowing.

"You are the love of my life," they both said simultaneously, realizing what they had always known.

Skip Simonds
Boothbay, ME

And then it was over. He knew it. His heart broke almost audibly. He was sure she had heard it. It was why she cried. It was why he hid his face from her.

The bright light burst through the window again.

The comet passed again...as it did 50 years before. He found himself once again in the bed of his youth with the love of his life. This time he knew that he was not the victim of her choices, but choices of his own. He knew that he could convince her to stay. But he knew now it had been better that she hadn't.

He let her sleep. He let her go.

There was no long healing this time. There was sadness, perhaps a deep melancholy. He knew it would abide, but it was the price he had to pay to walk the path he had originally been destined to walk.

He found his first wife again. They married as they had. They had the children they already had. Life was the same as it had been. It was also different.

His loss turned by stages from sorrow to disappointment to a scar called acceptance. It forever marked the spot of loss. However, he no longer carried the loss itself. He carried the joy of knowing he was in the right place at the right time doing the right things. He had lost nothing. He had gained everything.

He remembered for the rest of his life, this third time through, that last night before she left. He remembered it like one remembers the embrace of a beloved relative, long dead and missed, but no longer grieved. It did not have the sting of the first time they had said good-by. He remembered it as the last time they said good-by.

Sylvia Little-Sweat
Wingate, NC

Nova Scotia

Halifax lighthouse
shrouded in Peggy's Cove mist—
bagpipe elegies.

Sydney's Cape Breton
touts tall sculpted violin—
Gaelic gigs and jigs.

Anne of Green Gables—
revenant of Charlottetown—
Prince Edward Island.

Quebec City's crest
reached by steep funicular—
tall ship masts below.

Gulf of St. Lawrence—
whale in tandem cruising ship
spouting baleen spray.

Montreal's bright flags
wave Canadian farewells—
Maasdam docked in port.

P. C. Moorehead
North Lake, WI

Harsh Bedrock

The harsh bedrock of my reality scrapes against me.
My hands roughen; my arms bruise.

I claw at the endless steppe reaching out before me.
I hurt. I am dead.

Yes, dead. Yet I live.
Yes, I live.

Hands heal. Arms heal. I heal.
I stand. I walk. I live.

***

Patrick T. Randolph
Lincoln, NE

Soulmate's Silhouette

In an old photo,
Mom gazes out the window—
Her soulmate smiles back;

Dad's silhouette on the lawn—
Echoes of eternal grins.

Robert B. Moreland
Pleasant Prairie, WI

Southbound to Indiana Harbor

Cold night, wind chills the lake;
freighter a mile from shore.
Diesels pulse, engines bore,
waves ice dappled.

Ice mounds extend the shore,
mixed in with gritty sand.
Hours until port, land;
pilot house gleams.

To the north, Wind Point Light
flashes across Racine
guarding seaways between,
the flurries start.

Storm builds, snowflake ballet,
horizon disappears.
Radar faith, crews' worst fears;
pilot house fades.

Moreland, R.B. (2016) 2017 Wisconsin Poets' Calendar
"Southbound to Indiana Harbor" page 118.

Dorothy Hopkins
Waldoboro, ME

Coming Home

We knew Frank was going to die. We knew it in that vague, disbelieving way we all have when someone mentions death and taxes. Besides, he had nearly died four years before and then was given only six months to live. But we didn't tell him that because we knew he was tough. If he didn't have a deadline to meet, he would last longer than the doctors expected. Every day since then had been a gift. As Frank himself used to say after surviving 51 combat missions flying B-17s in World War II, "Every day above ground is a damned good one."

The January day I came home from work to find him dead in our bed, cold except for the spot that Corky, our beagle, warmed with his steadfast little body, I didn't cry. "Oh, that's it then," I said to him. He looked so peaceful in his sleep. I knew he had not suffered, perhaps hadn't even known he'd transitioned from nap time to eternal sleep. We should all be so lucky.

"We had a good run for it, didn't we?" Highlights of our nearly 30 years flickered in my head. Despite a 25-year age gap, we had a good long solid marriage. and two wonderful sons. I touched his stiff shoulder gently, still hoping his eyes would pop open and he'd say, "Checking to see if I'm still breathing, eh?" Then I tiptoed from the room so as not to disturb him.

I called the authorities to report the unattended death. After the ambulance crew, the state police and finally the hearse left the house, I brewed myself more coffee and sat down to make the inevitable phone calls. Stunned, our two sons kept saying they knew it could happen any day. They just hadn't expected it would be that day.

We had all been lulled into a false sense of security. When Frank was hospitalized just before Christmas, we were

Dorothy Hopkins
Waldoboro, ME

told his heart was functioning at 30 percent efficiency. He would probably go into kidney failure in the next few months. Thank goodness he was spared all that. I told the boys we had gone out to eat at their Da's favorite restaurant a couple of nights before. There were no indications he hadn't bounced back on the newly prescribed medications.

"Don't bother to rush home," I told them. "You were both here in mid-December and again at Christmas. We won't have any ceremony until spring when we can spread Da's ashes. I'll be all right. You know me. I always muddle through."

When I completed all the phone calls of immediate importance, I thought about bed and realized I could not sleep in our bed with Frank's absence still so present. I started upstairs. Then I remembered I had eaten nothing since breakfast, nothing but too much coffee in my system. I could neither eat nor sleep; instead, I lay there making mental lists of all the things I had to do in the next few weeks.

The next evening as I searched the kitchen for some comfort food, I heard footsteps in the shed. I reached the door just as our elder son opened it. He and his girlfriend had driven all the way from Massachusetts to our home in Wallagrass at the northernmost tip of Maine.

"I told you not to come."

"We needed to come."

The three of us, standing in a triangle, hugged and hugged. Within minutes, more footsteps sounded in the shed. There was our number two son. Now we had a circle of hugs. Frank always said they were both smarter than we were. With neither of them knowing the other was making the trip, they had, nevertheless, arrived within minutes of each other.

Only with them there did I realize how much I needed them with me.

Only together did we all begin to weep for the first time.

Rebecca Brooks
Topsham, ME

The Collective

A single, faithful snowflake
is such a delicate thing.
A clear and humble recipe
with one ingredient, King.
Imagine what would happen when
so many join the blissful fray.
A force of nature suddenly born—
a bright day of reckoning.
Today I will be a snowflake
as I gently touch the Earth.
And remind my fellow comrades
that our purpose is our worth.

***

Sylvia Little-Sweat
Wingate, NC

Chambers

Like the nautilus
souls—sequestered—dive the Deep,
rest beneath the reef.

Celine Rose Mariotti
Shelton, CT

My Uncle Dominic—An Old New York Yankee Fan

My uncle—Dominic Louis Iannotti
Born July 8, 1919
Left this world on March 9, 2010
He was a true-blue New York Yankee fan,
He never missed a game,
When he was young
He saw many a game
At the Old Yankee Stadium.
He taught me about baseball,
We went to see some Yankee games together,
I liked the Kansas City Royals,
We saw the Yankees play the Royals,
He'd watch a Yankee game on TV,
And listen to a Mets game on the radio,
Or whatever team was playing,
He was a multi-tasker, my uncle,
He'd read the newspaper at the same time,
While he watched the game on TV,
And listened to another game on the radio,
And he'd drink a glass of wine,
Oh, sweet Uncle Dominic,
I miss him so,
He must be watching the Yankees play
From up in Heaven,
My Uncle Dominic,
A true-blue New York Yankee fan.

San D. Hasselman
Boothbay Harbor, ME

Mutti

My mother was a character, and a well-loved one at that. Wherever we were, and we moved a lot, she made friends easily. Unbeknownst to me, she was a functioning alcoholic, which in hindsight explains a lot. My father was a teetotalling, straight up, Command Sargent Major in the US Army. Mutti had to hold down the fort by herself while my dad was deployed to Korea twice and to Vietnam twice. One year she had to go into the hospital for minor surgery. She experienced hallucinations from the anesthetic. I found the whole thing tres amusing, but it totally freaked my sister and my father out. Mutti didn't particularly like me, but I knew I was loved. She made no bones about it; she loved my sister, Pam, best. Well, during her hallucinations, she summoned Pam over to her and grabbed her by the collar and said two things that made me wet my pants. First she looked Pam right in the eyes and said, "I never liked you," and then, "I put all the money into the plumbing pipes." To me she said, "Could you go to the cabinet and get down a can of beans?" which turned me into an actress in *Our Town*, as I mimed getting down the beans.

At this point my sister and father were getting so upset they had to leave the room. Then she said to me, "Look, it's Robert Wagner in the doorway; go get him, he's here to take me out." Again, I did the *Our Town* bit, and escorted Robert Wagner over to the bed. I was then dismissed.

When I met up with my father and my sister, I said that it was wise to go along with the charade because by saying, "What the hell are you talking about?" would only anger and disorient her.

We three went back into the room. Then, Mutti, who fancied herself the Queen of Levittown, blew her nose into the sheets. I calmly said, "Mutti, we talked about this before you

San D. Hasselman
Boothbay Harbor, ME

came, you only blow your nose in your sheets in the privacy of your own home."

Gone were my father and sister. When I met them AGAIN, they both said, "What if she remembers all of this and thinks you are mocking her?"

To which I said, "I have nothing to lose, she doesn't even like me."

Six years later, when my father passed and Pam and I were cleaning out our parents' house, Pam insisted on searching the pipes.

***

P. C. Moorehead
North Lake, WI

Gushing

The rushing gust came,
gushing over the edges,
spilling over the sides.

The rushing gust came
gushing,
spilling,
rushing,
filling me with delight
and love
and hope
and joy.

I am loved, wanted.

I, grateful one, am gushing.

Peggy Trojan
Brule, WI

Crayons

In kindergarten, in 1937,
I could name all the colors
in my Crayola box.
Black, Brown, Yellow, Red,
Blue, Green, Orange, and Violet.
Colors unchanged since 1903.

My children had choices
from boxes of 24, 48, or 64.
Names like Denim, Robin's Egg,
Antique Brass, Tumbleweed,
Macaroni and Cheese, Outer Space,
or Razzmatazz, the winning entry
by a five-year-old in a naming contest.

Today, a child can choose
colors from a box of 120.
If they could identify 40 of these,
I believe they would qualify
for Mensa!

Karen E. Wagner
Hudson, MA

Fragility

I want to be more like
those salmon who fight upstream to reach
the broad fields of snow melt rivulets. Mighty
swimmers pile high in a heaving plane.
Pink spawning fish lay their eggs, fertilize
and bury them.
Eggs hatch, fry feed
adults fade pink to alabaster and die
with a purpose, all in good time.

I'm dawdling while taxis
and bicycles rush past me to be first
in line. I marvel the goodness of being alive
even if I get the back row seat
or my ice cream melts before
I check out. Salted sea breeze undoes
my hair. I hear young gulls cry
for their never-ending meal.
I lavish midday sun on my cheeks.
Lie me down in the interval between
rush hours in the jam of my pilgrimage
then leave me.

It's a long climb to my fifth-floor flat
a bit hard on the body.
I really should thank the owner, it's an easy way to go.
In all of my eighty years, I haven't felt my pain
relieved so well.
Darkness approaches.

Karen E. Wagner
Hudson, MA

It's my fragility I speak of.
Your experience might be quite different.
This delicate life better lived with few regrets
closing in a sweep of surprise near-
exits until the end.

***

Steve Troyanovich
Florence, NJ

dirge for an extinct planet

somewhere there must be
a tomorrow sheltered from pain
a place where dawn plays
with eternal rainbows of butterfly wings

Carol Leavitt Altieri
Lakewood Ranch, FL

The Myakka Savior

Elizabeth saved cattle and spent her fortune.
        to protect her part of the planet
and the watershed system...
        buying Triangle Ranch, natural Florida
where the Myakka River runs
        through swamps, below oaks and palms.
Many other cattle ranchers sold their
        thousand acres to circling developers.

We all know that water is life
        and water feeds the Gulf Coast where
the Triangle Ranch connects the Myakka River
        to the TatuI sawgrass marsh.
Here the Sandhill Crane family satiates freely.
        We must save the crested caracara, gopher tortoise,
and the Vespers of the Blessed Earth.
        A long dirt road wound through pastures,
some calves were missing legs from alligators.
        Finches, macaws, and larks create their patch.
racing against time.
        The flames of light fight off the shadows of hell.

Wendy Newell Dyer
Jonesport, ME

A Mother's Wounds

Standing on the summit of Katahdin on a cloudless day in September of 2014, after traversing up the notorious Knife Edge, I felt so small in the larger scheme of things. The climb up Katahdin was not just a physical feat, but also a deeply moving spiritual endeavor that brought healing to my mind and the cleansing of my spirit. The path that brought me to the mountain was a very long and difficult one, filled with many obstacles to maneuver, and various literal and figurative hills to climb. It was a journey that took me from a deep valley of despair and anguish to a place where I felt as if I were standing on the top of the world.

Two years before that sacred climb, I had received the kind of phone call that every parent fears getting. I was informed that my oldest son had been injured. His boss couldn't tell me if he was alive or dead but that I needed to get to Tennessee as soon as possible. I received the call in the curtain section of Wal-Mart in Ellsworth, Maine. I was getting supplies needed for the small garage apartment where I was going to live, in order to provide end-of-life care/companionship to my elderly adoptive parents.

I had just left my job at a local newspaper to return to my childhood home in Little Deer Isle. It was the island where I had been raised. My adoptive father was still at home dealing with mild dementia. My adoptive mother was in the throes of Alzheimer's. I wanted to be near the nursing home where she lived so that I could visit her daily. My adoptive father needed companionship and help with daily living.

That morning in September 2012, I had left my coastal home in Maine intending to put the finishing touches on my new abode. I had planned to move my belongings there the next day but I needed to finish up a few things. In the blink of an eye, my life took an abrupt turn toward the unimagin-

Wendy Newell Dyer
Jonesport, ME

able. It had started out as just an ordinary day, but by its end, I found myself standing in the trauma unit at Vanderbilt University Medical Center (VUMC) in Nashville, Tennessee, with my oldest son unconscious and hooked to a respirator.

After my son's boss had called, I was in a state of disbelief. I called him back to confirm what he had just told me. I immediately booked plane tickets. Living on the remote coast of Maine, I couldn't get a flight out of Bangor until five that evening. I spent the next two hours frantically trying to find out where my son had been taken, and if he was still alive. Eventually, I was able to speak with the detective in Oak Grove, KY, who had been assigned to his case. He assured me that my son was alive.

It was one of the longest days of my life, and one that I will never forget even if I tried. I clearly remember praying a great deal while I was in transit. I cried out to God and said, "You have taken my husband, please do not take my son too. Please don't take him now." It had been a little more than five years since my husband had died at the age of fifty-six, after a ten-and-a-half-year, nonstop battle with prostate cancer. At forty-two, I became a widow. I looked up and whispered to my deceased husband. I asked him to be with our son to keep him safe so that he might survive. I didn't think that I would recover from another death.

As our first flight landed in Detroit, the same questions kept going over and over in my mind, *Is this real? Is this some kind of a dream? This can't be real can it? Am I going to wake up? Did my son really get shot and assaulted*? All I wanted to do was to be with my son so that I could see for myself if it was true. The mind has a way of protecting itself when it has been bombarded by devastating news that shakes one at their core.

There was an internal battle to soften the jolting information that my brain was trying to process. I had some difficulty determining what was reality because that which I was confronted with was so disturbing that I didn't want it to be

Wendy Newell Dyer
Jonesport, ME

real. Time seemed to stand still and everything around me felt as if it were moving in slow motion. Little by little, I began to process it all and came to the realization that what I was experiencing was not a dream, but it indeed was reality. In that moment of realization, a wave of unfathomable fear washed over me. I was in a state of utter despair and filled with great anxiety.

There is nothing more frightening than to see your child in such a helpless and vulnerable state that a machine must breathe for them. It was shocking to say the least, so shocking that I made an audible gasp and covered my mouth with my hand as I said, "Jason. Oh Jason."

As I approached his bed, there was a hissing sound as a ventilator raised and lowered my son's chest. An IV line was in his arm, along with EKG leads connected to his chest, and a heart monitor beeping beside him. A catheter bag hung on the bed rail. An oxygen meter was clamped to his finger, and a blood pressure cuff was affixed to his arm. I immediately noticed a large cut next to his temple and dried blood in his hair. There were approximately ten or so neatly sewn stitches at the edge of his temple. I was startled by the indentation in his skull.

My son had been shot three times in the back, and had suffered a skull fracture from a forceful blow to his head next to his temple. It had left his skull splintered, much like if you had thrown a rock at a car windshield, or so his neurologist informed me. Over the next few days, they continued to assess his brain injury, checking for any swelling or changes in the brain through repeated scans and neurological exams.

Gunshot wounds, I was told, are some of the most horrific injuries to the human body. The damage that bullets and the friction that is created by them is extensive. Nerve endings and blood vessels are damaged, muscles are shredded and torn. Victims are left with gaping holes in their flesh that must heal from the inside out. Bones can be broken, shattered or splintered.

Wendy Newell Dyer
Jonesport, ME

Depending on what type of ammunition it is, there are fragments and pieces left in the body. Some stay there forever. Some move toward the surface and have to be removed. There is often blood loss and organ damage, and of course spinal cord injuries. Three bullets went into the right side of my son's back and passed near the spinal cord before making exit wounds on the left side of his back and side. Surprisingly none of his organs were hit, but they had left him with several broken ribs and had nicked his lower spine.

In a semi-conscious state, his first words after he came off the respirator were "Daddy, Daddy." My immediate thought was that perhaps my husband had heard my pleas and somehow he had been near our son and kept him safe. I also wondered if Jason had been so close to death that he had experienced the near-death phenomena of seeing loved ones who have died.

On the fifth day, the trauma surgeons felt that they could give him a near normal life. After the bone and bullet fragments near his spinal column were removed, they would stabilize his spine with rods and use bone grafts from human cadavers to repair the damage known as a laminectomy. If anything went wrong, he could have been left paralyzed.

We all celebrated the next day when he left the trauma floor to go to the surgical recovery floor. He would spend another week there as he continued to heal. A day after his surgery he walked for the first time since the shooting with the help of a walker. In the early days, I didn't know if I would ever see him walk again.

A little more than five weeks after that frightful morning at Wal-Mart, Jason and I began our drive back to Maine. The most traumatic part was behind us but the healing had just begun. For him, it would be months before he could resume normal activities. He wore a back brace for eight weeks to keep his spine stable as it was healing. It took him months after that to regain strength in his leg muscles, and to be able to move his back and torso to bend or lift. He had the physical wounds to recover from, while as his mother, I had emotional, spiritual and mental wounds that needed time to heal.

Though my only physical suffering had been from lack of sleep, I suffered immensely from mental and emotional distress from the traumatic event. I frequently had flashbacks. I was always looking over my shoulder as I was worried that the shooter might decide to come find us to finish what he had started with my son. I avoided large crowds. I didn't have much of a desire to be around people. The entire experience had turned my world upside down. How I saw the world and my place in it, changed dramatically.

My thoughts became bogged down with the realization that one human could inflict so much pain and suffering on another. I didn't know how to reconcile that in my mind. The part about my son's injuries and suffering that hit me the most was that all of his pain could have been avoided. The injuries were inflicted upon him at the hands of another human being. I had seen the worst of humanity when I looked into my son's wounds and viewed his injuries.

The following spring and summer after the shooting, I found myself becoming more and more obsessed with mountain climbing and hiking. I spent two or three days a week on the trails at Acadia National Park. The more that I hiked there, the better that I felt physically and emotionally. Being on a mountain brought me comfort because I was far removed from civilization, and depending on what trails I hiked, I could limit my interaction with other humans.

The woods had been my refuge as a child. I always had a strong connection to the land, ocean and the creatures of the natural world. My life made more sense when I was immersed in nature. I had always found healing there even as a child. Peace rested upon me whenever I entered the forest or when I sat by the ocean. I didn't always fully understand why I had that connection to the earth until I was twenty-five, and found my birth parents. It was then that I learned that I was a citizen of the Passamaquoddy Nation.

Wendy Newell Dyer
Jonesport, ME

When I started mountain climbing and hiking after my son's shooting, I thought about my Passamaquoddy ancestors. I often pictured them hiking and climbing in the same places where I found myself. I imagined how the landscape must have looked five hundred years ago. I wondered what their conversations would have been. I began to look at each hike and climb as a sacred endeavor. Many times I would bring an offering of tobacco to use before I started. I would sing familiar Passamaquoddy songs as I hiked and climbed. My healing came from my attempt to draw closer to the teachings and traditions of my ancestors, as I understood them.

The more time that I spent climbing, the less time I was thinking about everything that had happened in Nashville. The trees, ocean, mountains and wildlife were medicine to me. The world had no answers and little help for what I had been through. I found my answers and comfort in the high places where I climbed, far removed from the hustle and bustle of everyday life.

Each trail that I attempted became a ceremony to me. It moved past just being a physical workout. My hikes and climbs became spiritual experiences that helped me to slowly let go of the images and memories that were keeping me trapped in a life of fear and confusion after my son's attack. The higher I climbed, the freer I felt. In a chance meeting in 2014, while on a trail at Acadia, I met April Blair Carlson who was in her late sixties. We talked as we were coming back down the Precipice Trail, the east coast's most difficult, non-technical climb.

We began chatting about hiking and the topic of Katahdin came up. I told her that I was planning to do it again as soon as possible because fall was on its way. My new acquaintance told me that for three years she had tried to climb the Knife Edge but had to abandon her hikes each time because of rain, fog or wind. She was determined to try one more time. Less than a week later the two of us, along

Wendy Newell Dyer
Jonesport, ME

with her friend, found ourselves sitting at the gate of Baxter State Park just before sunrise.

That day I hiked ahead of them a number of times so I could sit alone for a spell on a rock until they caught up. I wanted to take in the scene fully. I breathed in the crisp air and felt the warmth of the sun on my skin. I became aware of all of the sounds and sights that I might have missed had I not taken the time to look in the four directions. I was moved to tears by the natural beauty that engulfed me. I knew I was experiencing one of my life's most sacred moments.

There was not a breath of wind on the mountain. The sky was so clear and blue that you could see for hundreds of miles in every direction. It honestly felt like I was sitting on top of the world. The weather was so perfect at the summit that we were in shorts and t-shirts. As we inched our way up the Knife Edge toward the summit, I felt happy to be alive, something that I had not felt since before that fateful day in September 2012.

I smiled and laughed so much all day that my face hurt. I was so far removed from those horrific hospital scenes that had plagued my thoughts for two years, and that I didn't know if I would ever shake. At the top, I left a small pouch of tobacco as my offering. Part of my reason for this expedition was because I wanted to symbolically leave my traumatic memories up on the mountain that day. I kissed the pouch, tapped my heart, looked toward the heavens, then hung it on the summit sign as we began the trip back down the mountain. It was late in the day so we knew part of our descent would be in darkness.

As luck would have it, of all nights to hike down Katahdin after sunset, we happened to pick the night of the full moon. I shall never forget seeing it shine on the mountain, creating such a beautiful silhouette of its peaks. It lit our path the last two hours after the sun had set. We stopped often to look back at the moonlit mountain peaks. When we reached the

Wendy Newell Dyer
Jonesport, ME

parking lot, I felt as if I was a different person than I had been that morning. I felt whole again after feeling so damaged and broken. It wasn't the end of my healing but it may have been the turning point.

I am still reminded from time to time of that dark period of my life. Now ten years after my son's attack, I have done my best to move on but I have moments when everything seems so fresh in my mind, especially after a mass shooting. There are days when I miss my former self, when I wish I could go back to my carefree days of innocence before the trauma, but then I remember to be thankful that my son is still alive and that we have recovered.

We both understand how truly fortunate that he was to have survived, and to now have a full and active life. If any of the bullets had been a fraction of an inch in any direction, he would have died or been paralyzed. If the blow to his head had been just a little closer to his temple, he would have suffered brain damage. Though it has been a long and often difficult journey to heal our wounds, we are the lucky ones. Many mothers across this land will not see their children recover from their injuries. Life has gone on for us, for my son. He is a walking, breathing miracle.

My son joined me at Acadia that summer after his injuries healed to help me train for Katahdin. The mountains also brought healing to him. We are both infatuated with mountain climbing, as are his two teenage sons that he is raising as a single parent. Finding joy in the mountains was one of the gifts that came out of the trauma. Some of my best memories of the past decade have been on a mountainside.

~Each day is a gift, a present ready to unwrap, to be enjoyed and celebrated.

GOOSE RIVER ANTHOLOGY, 2024

We seek selections of fine poetry, essays, and short stories (3,000 words or less) for the **22nd annual** *Goose River Anthology, 2024*. The book will be beautifully produced with full color cover in both paperback and hardcover.

You may submit even if you have been published before in a previous edition of the *Goose River Anthology.* We retain one-time publishing rights. All rights revert back to the author after publication. You may submit as many pieces as you like.

EARN CASH ROYALTIES. Author will receive a 10% royalty on all sales that he or she generates.

There is no purchase required and nothing is required of the author for publication. Deadline for submissions is April 30, 2024. Publication will be in the fall of 2024 (they make great Christmas gifts). Guidelines are as follows:

- Submit clean, typed copy by snail mail—**Mandatory**
- Email a Word (prefered), rtf, or PDF file (if possible)
- Reading fee: $1.00 per page
- Do not put two poems on the same page
- Essays and short stories **must be** double-spaced
- **SASE (#10 or larger) for notification—Mandatory** (one forever stamp) plus additional postage for possible return of submission if desired.
- Author's name & address at top of each page of paper copy and **first page of emailed copies**.

Submit to:
Goose River Anthology, 2024
3400 Friendship Road
Waldoboro, ME 04572-6337
Email: gooseriverpress@gmail.com
www.gooseriverpress.com

Printed in the USA
CPSIA information can be obtained
at www.ICGtesting.com
JSHW021947121123
51743JS00001B/73

9 781597 132626